Talk
to Me

Talk to Me

*A Therapist's Guide
to Breaking Through
Male Silence*

Kris Rosenberg

A Jeremy P. Tarcher/Putnam Book
published by
G. P. PUTNAM'S SONS
New York

A Jeremy P. Tarcher/Putnam Book
Published by G. P. Putnam's Sons
Publishers Since 1838
200 Madison Avenue
New York, NY 10016

Jeremy P. Tarcher, Inc.
5858 Wilshire Blvd., Suite 200
Los Angeles, CA 90036

Published simultaneously in Canada

Library of Congress Cataloging-in-Publication Data

Rosenberg, Kris.
    Talk to me : a therapist's guide to breaking through male silence / Kris
Rosenberg.
        p.   cm.
    "A Jeremy P. Tarcher/Putnam book."
    ISBN 0-87477-749-6 (hb acid-free paper)
    1. Men—Psychology.   2. Intimacy (Psychology)   3. Interpersonal
communication.   I. Title.
HQ1090.R69   1994   93-10362   CIP
305.31—dc20

Design by Mauna Eichner

Printed in the United States of America
1   2   3   4   5   6   7   8   9   10

This book is printed on acid-free paper.

Contents

Acknowledgments

FIRST, I WANT TO THANK *New Woman* magazine for publishing an article of mine, which was the seed from which this book grew.

To my agent, Elizabeth Zongker—my love and appreciation for finding that article and then finding me! She spoke those beautiful words: "Are you interested in writing a book on the subject?" *Was I interested in writing a book? Just since I was eight.* Conception took place. We became friends, moaning and celebrating together throughout the baby's development.

My appreciation, too, to Hank Stine, who believed in my idea, worked with me on the proposal, and sold it to Jeremy Tarcher.

I am deeply grateful to Jeremy himself, who took a personal interest in the manuscript in its early, embryonic form and all through its lengthy gestation. He was a presence throughout—in person, by phone, by letter. And he persisted in finding me a teaching editor who could handle my book-writing novitiate.

My everlasting gratitude to that editor—Dan Joy. Some editors tell a novice writer *what* to do; Dan taught me *how* to do it—with warm support, fine humor, wit, insight, and extraordinary brilliance. He took me by the hand . . . and heart. He often supplied the exact and beautiful phrase, with no concern for ownership. At this point, I'm not even sure whether some sentences are mine or his, or perhaps the creation of two quirky minds on long-distance phone at 3 A.M. Like a couple of parents, each of whom attribute all the baby's defects to the genes of the other, I'll just blame him for the bad parts.

Thanks to Daniel Malvin, whose phone calls from the office of Jeremy P. Tarcher, Inc., were invariably a lift, especially his jubilant, "I think we have a winner!"

And I thank Carole Volpe, my student at La Roche College, who looked up one day in class to say, "I have a name for the book: *Talk to Me.*"

I am grateful to the friends, students, clients, family—I cannot name you all—who listened to me, gave me insight and encouragement, and who inquired, as of a woman in her thirty-sixth month of pregnancy: "Isn't that book finished *yet?*" I hesitate to name anyone in this group—because by doing so, I necessarily leave out so many. Yet I must give special thanks to three:

To Harry, who acted as my Male-Point-of-View, who read drafts, bought me a big-screen Mac and taught me to use it, believed I could do anything, and made it financially possible for me to cut back on other work to write. He certainly gave me plenty of practice at breaking through male silence!

To my daughter Bonnie, who said exactly the right words—which I dare not repeat!—to enable me to write the *New Woman* article when I was in a body cast, recovering from a spinal fusion, being allowed twenty minutes each hour to sit at the typewriter, and collecting rejection slips. She provided hours of laughter at the grimmest times, contributed many of the examples in the book, and, as she put it, taught me to "get around in the patriarchy."

And to my daughter Aleta. On some of the heavy days, she said with good humor, "I used to have to make an appointment to talk to my Mommy, and now I can't *get* an appointment with my Mommy!" She was always with me though, taking me back and forth, seeing and hearing the worst as I went in and out of the hospital—once for cancer surgery—again and again during the writing of the book.

And, last of all, to those who gave me such misery that I had to write to show them.

Whatever the book is, thank heavens it's born.

ꙮ
Introduction:

From Isolation to Intimacy

Communication is the largest single factor determining what kinds of relationships [a human being] makes with others . . . how he manages survival, how he develops intimacy, how productive he is, how he makes sense.

Virginia Satir, *Peoplemaking*

MEN'S EMOTIONAL SILENCE IS the perennial feminine lament. Feelings of isolation pervade the relationships of innumerable couples; research has suggested that an average married couple talk to each other for about five minutes each day.

Any two people in a close relationship can fall into this well of silence. Since you are reading this book, you are probably trying to relate to a man who, regardless of your best efforts, doesn't disclose his feelings—at least to the extent that you desire. Even if you are a woman who tends naturally to draw out the confidences of others, you probably still experience, or have experienced, a sense of separation from the major man in your life. Male silence may have been the very reason you and your last partner separated.

What you have read previously may have discouraged

1

your efforts to bring about change. For example, a popular book for women features a chapter entitled "Why He'd Be Crazy to Open Up." The author advises that the expectations women place upon men in regard to verbal intimacy are unrealistic, and suggests that her readers turn to their female friends for "real depth of communication."

Numerous other experts urge couples to communicate in order to solve problems in their relationships—but offer little or no advice regarding *how* to do so. Sociolinguist Deborah Tannen, in her bestselling book *You Just Don't Understand,* recognizes that "the complaint most often voiced by women about the men with whom they are intimate is: 'He doesn't talk to me.'" However, as she clearly states, the purpose of Tannen's book is to describe differences in patterns of communication between genders, not to show her readers how such patterns might be changed.

My purpose in *this* book is to show you how to bring about such change. My personal and professional experience does not support the widespread pessimism about communication between men and women. I intend to teach you how to develop a verbally open partnership with your man—to help you transform your relationship from one of isolation to one of intimacy.

As a psychotherapist, couples counselor, teacher of psychology, and as a daughter, wife, mother, and friend, I have heard countless personal stories, and engaged in many close relationships. I have experienced how it feels to be left groping in the dark with regard to my male partner's deeper feelings. I have worked with couples in breaking through their barriers to verbal intimacy, and have participated in such breakthroughs with my own partner. These personal struggles have motivated me to write a book designed to help women who experience a sense of separation in their relationships and the men who have never experienced the release and healing in speaking of their emotions.

Some time ago I began to ask the question: what commonly prevents couples from experiencing intimate, deep, and revealing dialogue—the element most essential to a dynamic, fulfilling relationship? I looked carefully at what I had done professionally and personally to effectively bring forth emotional disclosure. I started asking men why they could not reveal their feelings and the results they experienced when they did open up. I asked them why they would talk to one person and not another, and especially why they might be closed about their feelings with the person they love the most.

I discovered that we as women often bring to communication with our male partners a set of principles quite different from those we bring to our interactions with others. Specifically, we are more likely to act as if we have a right to our men's thoughts. And while I initially supposed that women usually talk freely to their partners about feelings, I came to realize that most women, like most men, are not socialized to disclose emotion straightforwardly. We, too, often go through life in emotional solitude, separated from our lovers not only by their walls but by our own pretenses.

As women conditioned by social taboos against acknowledging our anger, we "band-aid" our messages of displeasure, cushioning our cutting words: "I know you didn't mean to, but . . ." And we dissemble with our men in various ways: faking orgasm, "playing hard to get," and "letting him win," behaviors which are all familiar components of traditional femininity.

We play such games in order to please our men, to avoid confrontation, to be more exciting and attractive, to circumvent rejection, and to gain approval, because we are conditioned to do so. These are some of the same reasons our men have for not being straightforward with us. In spite of our reputation for being entirely open, we are actually just closed in different ways. Men hide behind action; women hide behind "nice."

One of the major objectives of this book is to counter women's prevailing belief in the "otherness" of men. Women and men are not creatures of different species. Our interiors are more alike than our surfaces; we share the same basic emotions, but we are shaped to express—and repress—them differently. And to a great extent, the wall of emotional silence is maintained from both sides. This book will suggest ways in which, even with the best intentions, you might be inadvertently contributing to your man's reluctance to disclose.

Women and men alike may "skate across the surface" of relationships for fear that if we drop our disguises, no one could love us. Yet the opposite is true: *only* if we are known can we be loved for who we really are—instead of for an image we project. And while both you and your partner may fear that abandonment will result from exposing your feelings, rejection is one of the rarest consequences of emotional *denouement*. Couples are most deeply bonded when they self-disclose. And only by daring to risk the feelings of vulnerability that disclosure involves can we experience the truth that talking connects us.

Although we are often cautioned against "doing ther-

Myth
People commonly believe that if they allow others to know them, they will not be loved, and will perhaps be rejected.

Consequence
People tend to be afraid to let themselves be known, and this fear isolates them. By pretending, we are actually more likely to bring on that which we seek to avoid—rejection or abandonment.

Reality
The better you are known by your partner and the better he is known by you, the *less* likely you are to reject one another.

apy" with our partners, the art of healing through verbalization is not the exclusive province of psychotherapists.
Most of us obtain our "therapy" on a nonprofessional
basis from people with whom we are personally and
closely involved. We all constantly interact with each
other in harmful or healing ways, whether we stumble
along haphazardly or enter dialogue with forethought and
insight. And it is certainly preferable to pay attention to
the inevitable psychological intricacies of our relationships than to ignore them. Following the guidelines in
this book will help you and your partner to work in a
therapeutic way with each other. The caution against
"doing therapy" should be applied mainly to the tendency to take responsibility for each other's emotional
problems. Interacting in ways which facilitate healing
change is always desirable.

Myth
Popular opinion, supported by many "experts," maintains
that it is emotionally dangerous for you and your partner to
"do therapy" with each other.

Consequence
Believing that we dare not probe deep emotions with our
partners, we can actually do harm by our silence or naïve, un-
therapeutic approach. In any event, we lose the chance to enhance our relationships.

Reality
Most of us get our therapy in large part from the significant
people in our lives. Although professional therapy has specific requirements and conditions which are inappropriate to
the context of interpersonal relationships (and *vice versa*),
therapy in the sense of healing wounds and changing direction is well within the capacity of most couples. You can, in
fact, be very effective with the healing approach outlined in
this book.

During the process of writing, this book threatened to "run away with itself" and become a broad-ranging manual on relationships in general. For instance, many of the principles of communication discussed here apply equally well to relationships which do not take the form of heterosexual coupling—friendships, same-sex romantic pairings, family bonds, and professional associations. But space was too limited to deal specifically with such topics in this book. The subject of forgiveness also threatened to expand into a book of its own, but has been treated here in summary form in chapter eight.

Early outlines included an entire chapter devoted exclusively to dealing with anger, a subject which has now been integrated throughout the text; other books can serve as fine sources of further information on this topic, among them Harriet Lerner's *The Dance of Anger*. I had originally intended to include a chapter on infidelity and affairs, a subject which turned out to be impossible to contain so neatly; in this regard, I recommend Carol Botwin's *Men Who Can't Be Faithful*. I especially wanted to include a chapter which would aid women in determining if their partnerships were hopeless and should be abandoned; I wanted to discourage you, the reader, from concluding that you are responsible for your relationship and that you have failed. An excellent resource for addressing such concerns can be found in Robin Norwood's *Women Who Love Too Much*. Other highly recommended works in subject areas relevant to this book include Frank Pittman's *Private Lies* and Maggie Scarf's *Intimate Partners*.

The first three chapters of this book show what the wall of silence is like and how you can better understand your man and his patterns of communication, and provide you with the incentive, motivation, and optimism required for undertaking the project of deepening your communication. Chapter one, "He Never Talks to Me," examines the often hidden consequences of emotional silence and the sometimes unanticipated rewards of disclosure; it offers evidence that your man's need to talk about feelings is probably at least as great as your own. Chapter two, "Beneath His Mask," reveals the pain and fear that your partner's emotional silence may serve to protect, and chapter three, "Big Boys Don't Cry," explains the cultural and psychological conditioning that he must overcome in order to open up about his hidden feelings.

The place to start is always with yourself because *there* is your maximum power. When one component of a living system—in this case, an intimate relationship—is altered, that change catalyzes transformation in the entire system. While you cannot wave a "magic wand" over your partner, you can choose between inhibiting or actively facilitating his emotional disclosure. Thus, the chapters in this book that focus on practical advice emphasize *your* words and *your* styles of approach.

Chapter four, "Connecting," offers ways of creating an atmosphere of trust that provides a context in which intimacy can occur. Chapter five, "WordTraps," will guide you in identifying patterns of speech through which you may be inadvertently reinforcing your man's silence, while chapter six, "WordBridges," offers alternative approaches which encourage disclosure. Chapter seven, "Double Exposure," describes exercises for clarifying and enhancing communication in which you and your partner can actively participate. Chapter eight, "The Freedom of Forgiveness," previews the possibilities of transformation as you and your partner resolve issues of guilt and blame.

When an idea that runs counter to "popular wisdom" is introduced, it is highlighted by its appearance in one of several boxes that you will find scattered throughout the text. Within these boxes, you will find a statement of a "myth," or widely held belief; a statement of the negative "consequences" which often result from accepting the myth; and a statement of the "reality" or truth which contradicts the myth.

I offer this guide to the art of verbal touch in the hope that you and your partner can transform your relationship, moving from the agonies of emotional isolation to the deepest joys of intimacy.

&

CHAPTER 1

"He Never Talks to Me"

. . . But He Does Have Feelings

To communicate . . . is the most magic thing there is.
Gilda Radner, *It's Always Something*

There is a depth in the human psyche at which all feelings merge, and the disparagement of one constricts and dampens all the others.
Philip Slater, *The Pursuit of Loneliness*

Is YOUR MAN THE "strong, silent type"? Did he tell you more about himself in the first few weeks of romance than he has in all the time since? Do you long for the closeness you felt then?

Does your every attempt at talking about feelings end in a fight? Does your partner seem unable to express emotions other than anger? Have you become discouraged and decided to leave "well enough alone," even though you know your relationship is *not* well enough?

When you ask your partner how he *feels,* does he tell you what he *thinks?* When you ask him to talk to you, does he say, "I don't know what to talk about"?

Do you feel shut out because you never seem to connect with your mate? Do you feel unknown and unloved by him, and closer to your female friends than to him? Do you sometimes wonder whether all men are like your partner, or whether there is a special problem in your relationship? Have you tried everything you know to communicate, to draw him out—with no success? Do you try to understand him, while he seems determined to prevent it?

Do you feel like a client of mine who, after twenty-three years of marriage, told me, "There is no loneliness so bitter as lying in bed beside a man who has emotionally abandoned you"?

Although you are aware that you feel isolated from your man, you may not recognize the full extent and intensity of this lack of emotional communication and the seriousness of its consequences for you as well as your emotionally silent partner.

You may not realize that he suffers perhaps even more than you from the wall of silence behind which he hides from you. You may not be aware that he feels as intensely as you do, that he too needs love and belonging, and that his need to talk about feelings is as great as yours. You may not be able to imagine the joy that can be brought to both of you through emotional disclosure. And you may not believe that, in spite of past failures, there is great hope that intimate dialogue can flourish in your relationship—and that you have power to facilitate such change.

In the chapters ahead, you will learn how to bring these changes about.

Bad Things Happen to Closed People . . . and Their Mates

The cost of closing off between partners can be a dulling of sexual response in either or both, a blunting of joy, diminished power in the relationship, and sometimes even a decline in physical health.

Many therapists have found that problems of a supposedly sexual nature are almost invariably rooted in lack of emotional communication. Helen Singer Kaplan, an authority on disorders of sexual desire, compares trying to create sexual satisfaction without communication to trying to learn target shooting blindfolded.

The need for "someone to talk to" is also a major reason for affairs. The absence of feeling-talk may leave your partner—or you—more vulnerable to developing other romantic relationships.

Experts have long recognized that emotional disclosure is an essential component of well-being. Some psychologists define mental health at least partly in terms of the desire and ability to make oneself known to others (a practice which both requires and promotes self-knowledge). If we do not express what we feel, we take the risk of losing not only those we love but ourselves as well. Not telling may be not remembering, and not remembering is tantamount to forfeiting an aspect of our

11

Myth
Men have affairs because they are sexually dissatisfied.

Consequence
We may concentrate on the wrong areas in our efforts to keep our relationships monogamous.

Reality
Affairs more commonly start when one partner wants "someone to talk to." Often men have affairs because they need to talk and fear talking to their primary partners. Verbal intimacy leads easily to sex, which is one valid reason to create intimate talk with your *partner.*

being—the ultimate amnesia. As therapist and writer Sidney Jourard puts it, "When we succeed in hiding our being from others, we tend to lose touch with our real selves."

The cost of not communicating our feelings is isolation—a harsh, cold, psychological penalty. Prisons and military academies have long used isolation as punishment; offenders are treated as if they do not exist, made into invisible nonpersons. Certain families have their own form of solitary confinement: family members seek revenge by refusing to speak, to touch, even to make eye contact with one another.

Our culture is afflicted with emotional isolation, an alienation which contributes to our extraordinary rates of suicide, impotence, anxiety, depression, and addiction, as well as to a more subtle yet pervasive inner loneliness. We are prey to all manner of "stress-related disorders"—even though it is well known that one of the most effective ways to discharge stress is through verbal expression. (Even the term "stress-related" suggests that we relate more to stress than to other people.)

It may well be that the consequences of this isolation are borne more heavily by men than by women. Psychological disorders and physical diseases are more prevalent in widowed and divorced men than in women or married men. Widowers are more likely to die than widows or married men of the same age. Furthermore, social isolates—a predominantly male group—die earlier than those who have relationships.

According to psychophysiologist James Lynch, loneliness is one of the leading factors in premature death in this country, playing a role in "virtually every cause of death [be it] suicide, cancer, cirrhosis of the liver, automobile accidents, or heart disease." Each of these categories of catastrophe occurs with higher incidence among men. Men's repressed emotions do come out, sometimes in fatal forms; it seems that the less openly men relate, the more likely it is that their feelings will be expressed through personal disaster.

When days are dull and sex is routine, when a man feels lost and lonely, when life seems futile and meaningless, there is no automatic warning signal that lack of communication is the cause, especially if he is out of touch with his inner workings, as men often are. A man's defenses may be so solid that he isn't even aware of what the need to talk feels like. His conditioning to withhold may be so effective that acting out, rather than talking out, becomes an automatic response.

When he cannot comprehend why his life seems so empty, he may experience a vague restlessness, sexual frustration, or anger, rather than recognizing his need to be open. Feeling such elusive, indefinite emotion, he may move into bigger and fancier work projects, lose himself in recreational competition, or begin to hang out in bars, ostensibly looking for someone who understands him but actually making sure no one does. Finding that such activities fail to satisfy his undefined longings, he may resort to having affairs, changing his job, filing for divorce, leaving his family, or moving to another city. The ultimate result of his emotional silence can be bitter and devastating for both man and his partner.

A survey of relevant literature supports the popular belief that the male gender role stresses competence, self-reliance, control, and inexpressiveness of emotion. The evidence also suggests that fulfillment of that role brings increased risk of depression. To make matters worse, supercompetent men see their despondency as a sign of failure and, disguising their feelings, they may refuse help for their depression, which they cannot name. They may admit to sleeplessness, lack of joy, feelings of worthlessness—yet react with surprise when they hear, "Sounds as if you are depressed." Many American males are trapped in the paradox of having been taught to deny their own human responses, and then to feel ashamed of the misery that denial causes.

My work has brought me heart to heart with women unable to reach the point of mutual intimacy with their men, women who feel shut out, isolated, and alone. I have also walked the inner journey with men who have experienced such feelings of banishment, and I have seen that they have the same sense of isolation as women do. Surely neither men nor women truly want this kind of alienation.

In fact, men can be just as troubled by the walls of silence as women are. Without saying, "I feel lonely," the man in your life may actually be telling you precisely that, using words which do not match your expectations, or exhibiting behaviors you do not fathom. And you, while desperately in need of verbal contact, may miss the emotion he conveys altogether.

14

Men Do Have Feelings

A whole human being feels and expresses a full range of emotion. As sociologist Philip Slater, author of *The Pursuit of Loneliness*, says: "The emotional repertory . . . is simple and straightforward. We're built to feel warm and happy when we're caressed, angry when frustrated, frightened when threatened, hurt when rejected, offended when insulted, sad when abandoned, jealous when excluded, and so on. But every culture holds some of these human reactions to be unacceptable and tries to warp its participants into some peculiar limitation."

We often see this limitation clearly in our men. Commonly, the American male is culturally shaped to direct his emotion in very narrow, carefully defined channels that discourage outward demonstration of compassion and sensitivity.

Countless men have been able to conform so closely

to these sociocultural expectations that it is not always apparent to others that they even *have* feelings at all. For example, when I explained the topic of this book to a female client, she joked, "Oh, you're going to tell us why men don't have feelings!" Similarly, in a newspaper column, humorist Dave Barry advises women: "Do not pressure [your date] to share his most sensitive innermost thoughts and feelings with you . . . The truth is, guys don't *have* any sensitive innermost thoughts and feelings."

These humorous exaggerations skate across the surface of a tragic, deeper truth: in their effort not to show others their feelings, many of the most heavily conditioned men have lost the awareness that they *are* feeling. Thus, you may not know your partner largely because he does not know himself.

These silent men are rarely the cold, controlled, distant creatures they are stereotyped as being. Because many men typically act out instead of talking, they have acquired a reputation as unfeeling creatures. On the contrary, they simply express themselves less often by crying and talking and more often by hitting and performing.

Part of the alleged disparity in vulnerability between men and women derives from the fact that women are often more inclined to admit problems and are therefore more likely, as statistics show, to accept medical or psychological intervention. Many men, however, are reluctant to ask for assistance of *any kind,* as indicated by references in several recent self-help books to men who won't stop to ask directions if lost when driving. These references are the humorous tip of a deadly iceberg. That men go to psychotherapists and medical doctors less often than women is not an indication that men have less need. In fact, males, from childhood on, have a greater incidence of almost all behavioral and emotional problems. Men have earlier deaths from stress-related illness than their female counterparts, more suicide, and astronomically higher rates of homicide.

These are not the marks of people who don't feel. Even the strong, silent male is a person born with the capacity for the entire human repertoire of feelings. That such men have the complete human spectrum of emotion is made clear by their nonverbal expressions—from war to music, fierce competition to compulsive sex, self-sacrifice to art.

Because he neither converses with other men on an emotional level nor reads about their feelings, each silent man thinks he is different, that his reality is odd and unacceptable. We all see ourselves from the inside and others from the outside; we take people at "face value." Thus we compare our innermost feelings—and failings—to others' carefully painted masks. Seeking no response from others about his feelings, the silent male lives within himself, hiding his deepest sensitivities from childhood on.

A man may develop defense mechanisms to protect his psyche instead of learning how to talk emotions through. When his father died a few months after the death of his mother, a young man named Brett told me he would never let himself love one woman as much as his father did. As Brett saw it, his father died of heartbreak. Brett wanted many women in his life not because he was incapable of bonding exclusively to one woman but because he feared that he *would* do so—and lose her thereafter. He sought a backup system, "in case." (Such concern is not entirely irrational. As we saw earlier, a man's fear of dying as a devoted widower is statistically reasonable.)

We may have been led to believe that love is but one facet of a man's life, while it is the consuming passion for a woman. But many psychologists have observed that men generally fall in love more romantically than women, and are more likely to be thrown into depression when a breakup comes. Analyst Nancy Chodorow goes so far as to state that "men are not as emotionally important to women as women are to men," in part because a boy's primary attachment begins with a woman—his mother.

So we see that men do have feelings—very intense feelings.

Men Need to Love and Belong

It is unreasonable to assume—as our cultural stereotypes would encourage us to do—that women have an instinct for attachment and men don't, or that baby boys bond to women and grown men don't. A sense of belonging is the primary human drive, the essence of our being. This is true whether we are male or female, young or old.

As self-evident as this truth may seem to be, a quite different belief is commonly held. Abraham Maslow, pioneer of humanistic psychology, is well known for his theory of the hierarchy of human needs. This theory holds that we must satisfy our physiological needs (such as hunger) before we can afford to pursue psychological needs such as belonging.

Maslow is rarely challenged on this principle even though exceptions to it abound. For example, we can readily call to mind the famous diarist of the Holocaust, Anne Frank, who even as a child cherished her relationships above her own safety; starving composers who created great music; parents who died saving their children from burning buildings; heroes who, at the price of their own existence, plunged into frigid waters to rescue unknown others.

In contrast to Maslow, such outstanding thinkers as psychologist and writer Erich Fromm, theorist of human development Erik Erikson, and therapist Sidney Jourard assert the preeminent power of belonging as a primary human need. (In Fromm's view, belonging is even more basic than the needs for food and safety.) These writers—all males—speak, in one way or another, of the ability to bond deeply and authentically as a mark of maturity and wholeness and not—in the manner that the American cultural stereotype of masculinity would dictate—as a sign of weakness or "femininity" in a pejorative sense.

It is our innate nature, not "femininity," that compels us to attach to others. An infant alone will die; baby boys cling to their mothers as tenaciously as baby girls do. Both male and female infants can perish from lack of touch. Since our prehistorical beginnings, we have attached to each other for survival. We are social creatures; bonding is built into our genes.

The need to bond is at least as compelling for men as for women. But if men need to belong just as much as women do, why do men so often appear to lack this need?

The so-called "commitment phobia" exhibited by some men is taken to mean that they have no desire for long-term relationships. However, the real reason such

---

Myth

Popular belief is that it is not within men's nature to bond tightly, and that men's so-called "commitment phobia" means they have no *desire* for strong attachment.

Consequence

Both men and women in this society assume that the woman wants intimate bonding more than the man does; therefore, women devalue what they have to offer to men.

Reality

For men bonding is *at least* as alluring as hyper-independence, and as compelling as a woman's need. Some men desperately resist belonging to one woman because they fear their own overpowering urge to fuse with her, and, thereby, to become less "masculine."

men resist deep bonding is that they fear their own over-powering urge to fuse with a woman and thereby to become less "masculine" in the stereotypical sense. So, as much as they want bonding, heavily conditioned men also fear it. This culturally imposed image of masculinity is thus in deep conflict with a man's spirit, the nature of which is to crave belonging.

The reluctance of some men to disclose emotion and their tendency to struggle against becoming too close to any one woman are inextricably interrelated. Their ambivalence about intimacy is a major cause of their emotional silence, because they sense the connecting power of verbalizing feelings. They realize intuitively that intimate verbal touch is a bonding agent. They know that words are emotional connections, thought-links that blur the boundaries of personhood. And so they avoid talking.

Many men must endure shame for wanting to be emotionally authentic in a culture that says no to depth of intimacy and yes to the instant romantic fix. Yet most men are at some time in their lives involved in long-term romantic relationships, and marry at least once. Most of those who are widowed or divorced marry again. And often men do not leave one partner until they have another waiting. These patterns in male relationships offer convincing evidence of desire for belonging.

No less than women, men need to belong, to know and be known. This knowing requires emotional disclosure. Thus, because men need to belong, they also need to verbally connect.

Men Need to Talk About Feelings

Our deep desire is to love and be loved. All of us—men and women both—yearn to mingle our minds and hearts with those of another. We all need someone with whom we can share the inner layers of our being, who can participate in our sweetness, soothe our pain, and celebrate our triumphs. We need to find another to whom we can trust our fragile psyches. Only then, when another's spirit interpenetrates freely with our own, is our emptiness filled.

Talking about feelings is perhaps the most vital part of this kind of intimacy. Although we tend to think of emotional disclosure as a feminine characteristic, most men, when offered understanding and encouragement, and driven by the shared primal yearning for loving contact, will eventually find their way toward opening up.

Time after time in my practice as a therapist I have witnessed moving demonstrations that men are as capable of confessing deeper feelings as women. Her mate's emotional silence is often the problem thrusting a woman into therapy. When I ask such a woman if her partner will come in for a session, she almost invariably says, "He might come, but he won't talk."

Yet almost always—given an atmosphere of accep-

Myth
Men don't need to talk; talking about feelings is a feminine activity.

Consequence
Believing that men are by nature reserved about their feelings, we often give up on enabling our partners to open up.

Reality
Males need to talk about their emotions at least as much as females do. They sometimes appear to lack this human need only because they are programmed not to *talk about* but rather to *act out* a limited range of feeling. When they do talk, men are greatly benefited physically and psychologically.

---

tance and comfort and the knowledge that he will be understood—he *will* talk. If I can put him at ease, if his secrets aren't pried from him in the first session, he develops trust that he won't be betrayed. Sooner or later (usually sooner) he will begin to disclose his fears, his temptations, his sense of injury—all of his forbidden emotions.

I ask such a man about his feelings not only because *I* need to understand him but also because *he* needs to understand what he feels, to begin to see his own patterns and to *feel* understood. Women and men alike need to talk as a means of clarifying thoughts and emotions; talking reorganizes the mind.

When such a man unearths and talks through his deeply buried feelings, he almost invariably experiences the sensation that a burden has been lifted. When he has told the worst and it has been met not with judgment but with care and respect, and when his courage in telling has been acknowledged, he is usually as ecstatic as if he had suddenly discovered how to fly. One young man compared his feeling after his first therapy session to that of having had an "emotional blood transfusion." After vividly describing his humiliation throughout his ten-year marriage, he finished in amazement: "I can't believe I said all this stuff. I've never told anyone before!"

I cannot imagine going through life in such a closed condition; I would explode if I couldn't talk out most of my emotion most of the time. That is exactly what so many men do: they keep their feelings down for years, telling themselves it doesn't matter. Then one day all of the emotion erupts. They start doing things they've never done, things that are out of character for them, things that might never have happened if they had only been able to tell someone how they felt as they went along.

So, while men may resist talking about feelings, they have the need to talk, just as women do. However, unlike

21

women, men rarely reveal their inner workings to same-sex friends, recreational or work companions, even the best of whom may, in this competitive society, be considered rivals. As a man sees it, to talk about feelings is to give away the game, to reveal his own human weakness.

Like the legendary character who dropped a coin on a dark street and searched for it a block away because he could see better in the light of the street lamp, a man may attempt to achieve fulfillment of emotional needs without exposing the dark and hidden corners of his mind. This parable precisely portrays the man who seeks a certain kind of vital emotional sustenance where it does not exist—in drugs, games, or affairs, for example. Externalizing the problem, he takes some sort of action (as he has been taught to do) instead of starting to talk (which he needs to do).

When *talking out* becomes possible, the impulse to *act out* forbidden feelings is weakened. An extreme example: if a suicidal person can fully verbalize his or her pain and hopelessness, he or she is less likely to follow through with the act. It is not the feeling expressed but the feeling repressed, exiled to the furthest recesses of our minds, that undermines well-being and conscious will.

The Power of Personal Disclosure

So far this chapter has focused largely on the negative consequences we may have to endure when we *don't* communicate verbally about our feelings. These hazards, while compelling in themselves, provide only half of the picture. You and your partner can gain additional fuel and spark for undertaking the often difficult journey of disclosure by understanding the transformation of your lives that can be brought about by verbal touch.

While you no doubt anticipate that breaking through emotional silence will allow you and your mate to come to know each other more deeply, you may not have considered the extent to which each of you will come to know *yourselves* more deeply as well.

Contrary to the fears of many (especially many men), the closeness that is brought about by revealing ourselves through talk does not submerge our fundamental identities. Rather, talking enables us to perceive and solidify that identity. Through intimate verbal touch, we *discover* and more fully *become* who we really are.

Self-disclosure and self-discovery are inseparable, each leading back to the other. Therapist Sidney Jourard—who describes therapy as a process of becoming "more transparent" to oneself—says: "No [one] can come to know himself except as an outcome of disclosing . . . to another person." Thus your partner's talking not only will enable *you* to know what he thinks; it will enable *him* to know his own thoughts in a new way.

Emotional dialogue offers many other significant and lasting rewards for each partner individually and for the relationship:

23

- The enormous emotional energy required to keep threatening feelings concealed can be released. Freely expressing emotion fires us with energy, excitement, a rush of adrenaline. There is a kick in self-discovery, an excitement in the risk we take when we dare to become vulnerable to each other.
- An intense emotional breakthrough infuses a stale relationship with a renewed sense of fun, romance, and passion. For couples with sexual dysfunction, the famous sexologists Masters and Johnson have long prescribed the verbal exchange of vulnerabilities.
- To fully integrate our own thoughts and feelings, we need to articulate them. By talking with each other, you and your partner can gain new perspective and fresh vision.

Expressing ourselves verbally allows us to see

patterns that remain hidden in emotional silence. Once we reframe a problem, we begin to perceive it anew, to become receptive to the bits and pieces of information—the associations—we have previously been unable to see. In this way, verbal expression creates new thought patterns. Time after time, a client laying out a problem will say, "Somehow I never thought about it that way before." He didn't think the thoughts until he heard his own words!

- When we open our emotional gates, we generate problem-solving alternatives. In Taylor Caldwell's novel *The Listener,* people bring their problems to an unseen listener who sits behind a curtain. As they speak, the listener never utters a word in response. Yet slowly each speaker unravels thread by thread the tangle of his own story and leaves with a fresh vision of possibilities. As the reader realizes before the story is finished, there is no one hidden behind the curtain. Talking itself leads the characters to solutions.

- Articulating our pain can actually enhance our health. Although the exact biochemical mechanism is not yet known, studies indicate that emotionally describing upsetting experiences can stimulate the immune system, which is often depressed by loss and trauma. Current research offers evidence that verbal exploration of traumatic memories may result in a significant boost in levels of T-cells, which play an important role in immune function. According to psychophysiologist James Lynch, "Human dialogue not only affects our hearts significantly, but can even alter the biochemistry of individual tissues."

In an old story, a journalist, when asked his opinion of a political matter, replies: "How can I know what I think until I see what I write?" How can we know who we are until we hear what we have to say? By providing us with such an opportunity, other people can become the mirrors of our souls.

"Do I Have the Right to Try to Change Him?"

You may ask: "Doesn't my partner have the right to be whatever he is?" Of course, and the choice, whether to expose his inner being, is ultimately his own. This book is not *against* men, not an instruction manual for dragging them kicking and screaming into confessions.

However, having been conditioned to be closed about his feelings, your partner deserves a chance to see how the process of open communication works, to realize that it *does* work, to see how his life and your relationship can be transformed by open expression of feeling, by authentic verbal contact between you. While we each have the right to our own choices, no one makes a choice in a vacuum. In a culture which negates his natural need to verbalize emotion, you can become a counterforce for expression of feeling.

With good reason, your man may resist a blatant attempt to change him. With equally valid reasons, you may resist any implication that you have contributed to the situation, to lack of verbal contact in your relationship, that once again it's up to you to provide the solution for an interpersonal issue. The fact is that you are the one most aware of the pain his closedness inflicts upon you and upon himself, of the harm to your relationship. You would not be reading this book if you were not interested in talking, in making your relationship the very best possible.

In making the effort to do something about a problem, you become highly visible. The one who is trying to change something is the one usually accused of making mistakes. The players on the bench are never blamed for team losses. Men and women are very different when they are being drawn under by psychological currents; *women tend to signal, while men pretend to swim.* A man may deny that anything is wrong while a woman attempts to initiate change. "Can This Marriage Be Saved?" is *not* a feature of *Sports Illustrated!*

You cannot wave a magic wand over your partner; you *cannot change* him, but you *can* choose between blocking or facilitating his potential to move from isolation into intimacy—which, of course, moves you into intimacy as well. You can become an affirmative enabler, a part of your man's formative milieu without compromising your own integrity and without invading his rightful autonomy.

He Needs a Gift That You Can Give

Recognizing the power and importance of intimate communication can help us to affirm our own power and importance as women, for in this arena women traditionally have been considered to have exceptional skill. Whether or not it is so by nature, a special sensitivity to the inner life of others is a feminine talent; feelings are our language.

Unfortunately, in a society which places excessive priority on material riches, many women tend to underestimate the value of our special gift for relationships. We buy into the "beauty-gives-us-sex-gives-us-someone-gives-us-dollars" scheme, and, particularly when we are not stereotypical beauties or we have aged beyond our most seductive years, we lose sight of our priceless power to sustain intimacy. If we feel one-down, helpless, or excessively dependent upon our men, the venture of openness becomes too risky.

We must remember that our men do not love us because they perceive us as perfect; they love us because of the way they feel about themselves when they are with us. Only when we fully realize our extraordinary ability to provide a sense of belonging can we find the courage to open up deep communication. Only when we fully comprehend how each man actually hungers for attachment and belonging—even though he may also be fearful of them—can we be more confident in what we have to offer. To begin the journey of emotional dialogue, we need to be in touch with men's deepest needs and with our own inherent value.

Men have far fewer culturally approved outlets and opportunities than women to share real feelings. A woman usually will confide in a friend. Men, for the most part, don't offer their mysteries to other men. When lost, confused, or depressed, women are also more likely than their male counterparts to enter therapy, an avenue of exploration and healing which is still considered off-limits for American males. Therapy is, at least to a large degree, considered among men a sign of weakness. Case in point: in the 1992 presidential campaign, one side criticized the opposing candidates for having had family counseling, claiming that "real men don't lie on the couch." With this false image to struggle against, men need women all the more to provide a sense of belonging.

Communication is not only a means; it is an end in itself, a form of intimacy. It is not a process of suffering you must go through in order to arrive at intimacy; rather, it is a kind of lovemaking—whether gentle, painful, or passionate—a joyous dance occurring within a context of continual connection.

Children dance until they're taught that they don't know how to "do it right" and that proper dancing must be learned. A major block to the free and spontaneous, even childlike, rhythm of communication between you and your partner may be that you are dancing in a masquerade. To free your man to disclose his emotions, it is necessary to reach the real person hidden beneath the mask.

In the next chapter, I will discuss the masks men wear to conceal their vulnerability. When you learn more about these disguises, you will see how they actually disclose the faces they hide. Thus, looking at the masks your man wears can become a first bridge to his authentic self.

CHAPTER 2

Beneath His Mask

Discovering His Hidden Pain and Fear

We are more profoundly united by our common humanity than separated by gender . . . We are as incurably romantic as women. [But] silence is manly . . . Better a heart attack than speaking openly about a broken heart.

Sam Keen

IN AN ARTICLE IN *Ms.* magazine, writer Gilbert Deering Moore vividly describes a man's disillusionment with the macho masquerade. He recounts, as only a man could, his path to maturity through awakening awareness and sensitivity. Moore gives us a privileged glimpse behind the masks our men have had thrust upon them by cultural expectations:

> A man with a broken heart is in big trouble. There's no place to go with his humiliation and his tears. His he-man friends will laugh at him. A man has no business crying in the first place . . . this is what my Daddy might have said, had I been silly enough to unburden myself at his feet.
>
> [A man] wants to be known as a great lover, but by this he means not someone who feels deeply, but someone who [is proficient in the sex act]. His preoccupation is not love in the heart but technique in the head.

Moore goes on to describe how much his acceptance of the stereotypical masculine role cost him:

> On the surface I'd been having a grand time sleeping in all those beds, but behind the mask [was] a face contorted in pain . . . being a man conditioned to keep out of touch with feeling, I'd been a stranger to . . . my innermost self.
>
> The endless pursuit of pleasure does not in the end bring pleasure . . . quite apart from his brain and his broad shoulders and his big bamboo, a man [has] a heart every bit as fragile as a female's—quite often, more so.

Like so many men in our society, Moore had been wearing a mask, a defensive façade which concealed his wounds and covered his fear and pain. Men who wear such masks have been conditioned to think that in order to gain approval they must act as if they are what they are not. But, in truth, the mask is rarely as lovable as the face it disguises.

We all use masks to some extent to help us carry on public interactions and to render our inner conflicts outwardly manageable. However, while women also masquerade, we are perhaps more ready than men to drop our masks when we recognize feelings of isolation and the need to make verbal contact.

By contrast, a man's mask is often an external manifestation of deeply entrenched internal defenses. Such a mask serves to shut a man in as well as to shut others out, to keep him from facing his own normal feelings of weakness, failure, and dependency, which he has been conditioned to consider intolerable flaws. A masked man needs to accept these natural emotions, which he pretends not to have, and to know that his intimate partner accepts them as well.

Since so many American men tend to be "Lone Rangers," in order to relate to them, we need to consider the crucial question, "Who is that masked man?" We cannot connect with the man beneath the mask by direct attack. We must circumvent his emotional shield and deal not with his defenses but with the pain and fear those defenses conceal.

Understanding his mask and the subtle ways it hints at what lies beneath can provide you with ways of going around his defensive silence. By developing a sharpened perception of his hidden emotions, you can begin to communicate with the person rather than the *persona*. Instead of seeing a mask which shuts you out, you can see the fear which shuts him in. It is as if, like the fairy-tale princess, you can learn to see the prince within the frog. The princess first had to perceive what the frog really was before he could appear as his genuine self.

Therapist Sidney Jourard has written that "Some men are so skilled at 'seeming' that even their wives will not know they are lonely, anxious, or hungering for affection." Jourard's implication is that while women are skillful at tuning in to the feelings of others, men are even more skillful at acting.

While masks do have a great deal to tell us about the men they hide, there is no simple one-to-one correspondence between a certain type of mask and the feelings that lie beneath it. A particular mask can hide a wide variety of emotions. For example, one man may conceal painful truths because he genuinely cares about your feelings (almost all of us have at one time or another done the same with someone we love). Another feels he can't be a decent person if he hurts you ("It isn't right—boys don't hurt girls"), while yet another wishes to avoid confrontation.

Similarly, one underlying emotion can be covered by various masks, just as one frightened dog bites while another cowers. Masked men rarely wear just one disguise; they may switch masks according to the situation. (And in moments of sublime security, they may forsake the masquerade altogether.)

Until your partner begins to verbalize his feelings, you cannot be certain what lies beneath his mask. Initially— before the process of communication is well along—you may need to dig, to analyze, imagine what his emotions *might* be, in order to stimulate enough back-and-forth to bring out his authentic being.

I would caution you in doing this to avoid categorizing your man, and suggest that, considering all of these clues, you examine the possibilities you are faced with in your unique partner. My intention is to help you consider whether your partner might be wearing certain masks, and to offer an understanding that uncovers his hidden pain and fear, to which you can compassionately respond.

Countless times I've heard women say things like, "I know there is a loving man in there—if only I can bring him out," or "When I look at him, I can see that little boy still inside him." The images we sometimes have of those sweet and sad little boys are often quite real. Yet the men before us often have learned to suppress their softness beneath a mask of bravado. Once you are in touch with his vulnerability, you can express your own compassion.

Fears, Needs, and Traits Common to the Masks

Certain drives and emotions thread through almost all masks. A basic pattern, an intermingling of fundamental human feelings, operates to some extent in every psyche. We differ in how these emotions configure and how we express them; we all possess every note in the scale, but we play our own unique melodies. (Men and women sometimes play in different keys.)

An ordinary fear or need can become exaggerated into self-limiting, self-defeating forms. For example, it is natural, even healthy, to feel frightened when threatened, but to be perpetually afraid because one was once threatened is a mark of deep anxiety.

Masks conceal such exaggerated forms of various emotions, needs, traits and behaviors. Although other, more specific, characteristics are later presented along with each specific mask, described below are several features common to most masked men. Keep in mind that any characteristic which includes fear of love or attachment also inhibits feeling-level talk, which is a bonding agent.

FEARS

1. Fear of love as misery

Women sometimes inadvertently promote these fears in men by portraying what I call the "sacrifice model" of love. When a man sees a woman "coming apart" over the loss of a romantic partner, he can only see love bonds as conducive to misery. Her behavior may reinforce a message he received as a child from parents who were supposedly "in love" but were nonetheless clearly unhappy in their relationship.

Perhaps because we feel loved if our men need us, women often believe their extreme upset in the face of rejection will convince their partners of their deep devotion. This tactic doesn't work. Often, when a man flees, he isn't concerned about whether his partner loves him. In fact, he might feel safer within his psyche if she loved him a little less.

2. Fear of being loved

Women often think that men who avoid attachment do so because they are afraid to love. Sometimes, however, such men are more afraid of *being loved*. Being loved is an X ray of the soul in which masked weaknesses can be revealed. A generally fearful man may thus equate being unlovable with safety from such exposure of the psyche.

If he *loves,* at least he has some control: he can measure

Myth

We think if we show intense emotion, such as crying, our men will realize how much we love them and respond.

Consequence

Women—however inadvertently—too often act out what I call the "sacrifice model of love." Regardless of your deepest yearnings to be loved (or, perhaps because of them), you may reinforce a man's fear of attachment by role-modeling love as misery: "See how I suffer because I love you so much." Men look at us, the "experts at loving," and, seeing what torment loving has brought us, vow never to allow themselves to be that vulnerable.

Reality

Men usually do not see our agonizing as proof of love, but rather as a sign of the terrifying vulnerability love brings.

Consequence

They deliberately try to avoid becoming too deeply in love.

---

out what he gives, setting limits. But, as he sees it, if he opens himself to *being loved,* he might lose himself altogether, having no power over what pours into him.

Therefore he leaves no opening into which love can flow, and consequently no channel for intimate verbal contact. Ironically, the one most in need of love is sometimes least able to receive it.

3. Fear of abandonment and rejection

This fear is one of the most primal, fundamental, and universal motivations in the human psyche. The built-in anxiety that both men and women share about not belonging, being left out or left alone, does not disappear with maturity. Paradoxically, some masked men may not allow themselves to belong to anyone, in order to protect themselves from the possibility of being abandoned—and from the pain such rejection would involve. As explained in chapter one, this is the motivation that often underlies the ambivalence of the so-called "commitment-phobic" male.

4. Fear of being unworthy

If he feels unworthy, he may exhibit a cluster of behaviors and thinking patterns:

- He may treat you unkindly, cutting you down, so that you feel as insecure as he does. Having characterized you in this manner, he may then find it difficult to allow himself to love you. Feeling unworthy himself, he may assume that you must also be unworthy, since only a deficient person could love him. These consequences fuel further unkindness on his part.
- If he *does* allow himself to see you as a worthy person, he still may not allow himself to feel truly loved by you. Because he views himself as unworthy, he assumes that your love must be directed toward a false image of him. Since he believes you would never love him if you found out who he really is, he makes sure to keep his mask tightly in place.
- He withdraws from you or actually leaves you, protecting himself from what he believes is your inevitable rejection of him by rejecting you first.
- He confronts your love with disbelief: "You don't love me, you just want to use me," or "You just feel sorry for me."

5. Fear of return to infantile dependence

He fears that, if he dares to love, he will regress to the symbiosis of early childhood. His original identity was formed by sacrificing his total infantile fusion with mother. To become a "real man," he was forced to relinquish a portion of his closeness to her.

The metaphor of the boychild tied to his mother's apron strings is colored with connotations of shame and helplessness; such a child is made fun of by other boys. He fears that, if he again bonds to one woman who provides sustenance, he'll again be like a child—vulnerable, controlled, and in bodily jeopardy if he should lose her. Because he knows, at least intuitively, that deep exchange of feeling leads to bonding, he keeps his mask solidly in place to avoid such bonding and maintain the independence of his hard-won "masculinity."

6. Fear of being "feminine"

In our culture, being "all man" requires forgoing feminine characteristics. Males in this society are often defined in terms of what they are *not* instead of who they *are*; not what they *do* but what they *don't* do—like show tender emotion. Their excessively "masculine" mask may require that they refrain from intimate dialogue, traditionally a province of femininity.

7. Fear of an emotional "scene"

Anxiety about others' emotional displays is probably an inborn response. Very young children react with obvious dismay when they hear another child cry, and many animals respond with alarm to other animals' wails. However, the dread of others' emotionality is intensified in those of us who in childhood were exposed too frequently to our parents' distress. (While women also share this anxiety, men are more likely to have been taught to mask it as a sign of weakness.) A man may incorrectly assume that avoiding honest dialogue will spare him from being exposed to the threatening emotions of others.

NEEDS

Masked men have the same basic needs common to all human beings. Since these needs will therefore be quite familiar, they will be reviewed here quite briefly. However, in considering the psyche of the masked man, it is important to remember these needs because masks often conceal some of them so effectively that we may not even be aware that our men have these needs at all.

1. The need for belonging, nurturance, tenderness, bonding, love, and intimacy.
2. The need to be authentic, to express one's real self (including vulncrabilities) without having to fake or pretend.
3. The need for peer acceptance, approval, and admiration.
4. The need for success, achievement, and accomplishment.
5. The need for privacy, which, when exaggerated, can evolve into the habit of secrecy.
6. The need for pleasure, ranging from sexual fulfillment to the joy derived from a job well done.
7. The need for independence, for the freedom to make the choices that determine the course of one's life.
8. The need for safety, security, consistency, and continuity.

Masks often exaggerate those needs which fit the stereotype of masculinity in order to conceal other needs which are considered signs of weakness or femininity. For example, the need for independence may be overemphasized as a means of hiding the need for belonging. Young men often suffer the derision of peers when they announce that they are in love, while winning admiration for recounting tales of collecting sexual "hits" or "scores." This kind of social pressure encourages the development of a mask which displays the need for pleasure while concealing the drive for belonging (a distortion which develops in order to meet the need for peer approval). And when the need for belonging is masked, intimate communication will suffer.

TRAITS AND BEHAVIORS

1. The masked man may hand you a quick solution to a problem or issue with which you present him, and thereafter consider the matter closed.

He does not believe that talk has functions other than problem-solving. When you want to discuss a situation about which you have strong feelings, he is inclined to offer a fix—"You should quit the job you hate," "You shouldn't let your mother get to you," "You should see a doctor if you're tired"—bypassing the need for further discussion.

2. It may appear that he believes you can "read his mind."

To some men, the intuitive powers of their partners seem to verge on clairvoyance. (Since he lacks skill in expressing his feelings, this distorted view may provide his only means of believing that he is known—a belief necessary to his sense of belonging.) He may be comforted if he sees you as tuned in to his needs, but he will be disconcerted if he feels he is being mentally invaded. In either case, he may not see the need to discuss his emotions because he unconsciously assumes that you *already know.*

3. He may have a rich fantasy life which he confuses with reality.

Men are discouraged by society from being in touch with certain aspects of reality—particularly the reality of their own natural fears, needs, and limitations. Reality becomes replaced with a more macho version of their own inner and outer lives, which they often brag about in conversation with other men. Too much soul-baring dialogue would tend to threaten this fantasy existence.

4. He may be excessively ambivalent.

All of us have multiple, often contradictory, emotions. We all experience a range of feelings toward our partners, which from time to time conflict with one another. These natural, normal feelings become magnified in masked men. As a result, they may experience anxiety created by internal conflicts.

A man may believe he is disclosing the whole truth about his feelings. However, the extremely ambivalent man cannot, in fact, tell the truth. For him, there *is* no truth about emotion—rather a constantly shifting kaleidoscope of fragments, broken pieces of ideas and feelings.

In the discussions that follow, you will see how the fears and needs discussed above simmer in conflict beneath the mask, giving rise to this sometimes paralyzing ambivalence—which for you may be your masked man's most frustrating trait. For instance, the man behind the Co-independent mask is ambivalent about abandonment versus suffocation. The Sweetheart suffers from a conflict between wanting to behave in a loving manner toward you and his need to express anger, which has been stifled. The Dreamer is ambivalent because, while he needs to be himself, he fears that his real self is inadequate. The Hero is divided by his need to be "masculine" and his need to express feelings of tenderness. The Defender desires you, but fears your power.

The Masks

You may be able to identify one or more of the following masks as typical of your man, although no actual person will conform perfectly to any of these images. The discussion of each mask begins with a brief overview, followed by a description of the behaviors and patterns of interaction associated with it and the feelings you are likely to have in response. Then follows an exploration of the emotions a man may be concealing beneath his mask and the underlying needs he may be driven to pursue.

Each section closes with a look at the particular vulnerabilities which might lead each masked man into an affair.

The purpose of describing these negative-appearing images that men project is only to show the emotions that they hide. Remember, as you read about each mask, you will find beneath it a human being with fear and pain who has been taught to cover his feelings.

THE CO-INDEPENDENT

Overview

Quite the opposite of the "co-dependent" of recent fame, whose compulsion to rescue her partner reaches far beyond the bounds of healthy interaction and interdependence, the Co-independent fervently avoids close entanglements. One client of mine described Co-independence with the exclamation, "I'll tell you what's sicker than being co-dependent—thinking you can be totally independent of everyone!"

The Co-independent's major fear is of being fused with you. A Co-independent is unpredictable, inconsistent, and often refuses to make plans. He alternately pursues you and distances himself from you. He has dual masks: one which smiles as he chases after you, and one which goes blank as he vanishes. You are confused, crushed, attracted beyond your better judgment, and hypersensitive to his subtle signals of forthcoming emotional and behavioral change. When you bring up a source of tension between you, he may say, "That's just how I am." He tends to be vague and secretive. Your friends may say, "When will you have enough of that man? You don't deserve this."

What he does and how you feel

In the beginning you are tantalized by the charm and urgency of the Co-independent's courting as well as by your vision of the person hidden beneath the mask. You are seduced by your own desire to bring out the best in him; he is an intriguing challenge.

The Co-independent may have observed an unhappy truth: men who are elusive and "smooth" are more attractive to some women than men who are honest, kind, and considerate. As one young woman cleverly put it, "I have a date with a nice man. You know how I know he's nice? Because I'm not attracted to him."

Sometimes the Co-independent seems to be "lost in his own head" with that "faraway look in his eyes." If you ask what he is thinking, he says, "Nothing." You are constantly trying to figure him out.

Sometimes when you appear in a new outfit, you feel awkward because he seems not to notice. Nonetheless, you hear him compliment other women on their clothing and appearance. He might even tell you how beautiful another woman looked.

The Co-independent continually sends equivocal messages. His body conveys one meaning and his words another; he says one thing today and something else tomorrow. When you confront him about something he does, he insists that he is doing something quite different. He keeps you off balance; you drive yourself crazy trying to make sense of his inconsistencies and the contradictory feelings he expresses. You may begin to doubt your own perceptions.

If he talks about what fun the two of you will have on a cruise in the distant future, during the same evening— or even in the same breath—he warns that he "isn't in the relationship for anything long-term." He frequently says, "I'm not cut out for marriage," even if the subject hasn't come up. (However, your Co-independent may, in fact, marry you, frightening himself into sudden emotional withdrawal that can manifest, for instance, as single-minded concentration on his career.) Like a tacky commercial interrupting the best scene in the show, he is in effect saying, right in the middle of the real thing, "This is great entertainment, but the curtain will come down soon."

The Co-independent is tentative about advance arrangements. He may almost wince in response to remarks you make regarding plans, even for events as innocuous as the next evening's dinner. He may be vague beyond the point of privacy about his reasons for avoiding such simple commitments, becoming secretive, mysterious, and evasive about his own comings and goings. "We'll see what comes up," he may say, "I don't know what I'll be doing," or "I think I'm doing something else tomorrow night."

He is particularly reluctant to accompany you—or to have you accompany him—to family functions such as weddings and holiday celebrations. Even after years of presumed partnership, he may still attend important events alone. (He fears that your appearance with him at such gatherings might solidify his bondedness with you in the eyes of others.)

The Co-independent has such quick changes of heart and mood that he may suddenly disappear for periods of time. He is most likely to withdraw abruptly when you feel that things have been going particularly well between the two of you (or when you feel that you especially need him). You are left wondering what land mine you stumbled upon. You spend a lot of time mentally reviewing the details of your last time together, the conversations, the lovemaking. You may ask yourself, "Was it something I said?" In truth, the fact that things actually *were* going well between the two of you was precisely what inspired his fear.

There may be an uncanny timing to the Co-independent's return from such absences. A female character in Michael Dorris's novel *A Yellow Raft in Blue Water* says of her lover, "Just as I was recovering from his last disappearance . . . [he reappeared]. He had radar that sensed my breaking point. One more day alone and I could [have shrugged] him off, but he never gave me that chance."

You may keep trying different strategies in hopes you'll discover the key to keeping him close. The paradox for you is that the dearer you become to him, the more he will struggle to escape. Conversely, if you say that you are confused by his behavior and think you must break up, he says very little—but suddenly becomes more excited about your relationship.

When you are dancing around the fears of a Co-independent, you find yourself falling into patterns of pretense. How can you be open about feelings which terrify him? You learn to deny your own needs in an effort to assuage his insecurities. You may develop a superficial relationship wherein both of you are closed and inauthentic in your communication.

Beneath the Mask

The Co-independent flees from you as soon as *his own* impulse to cling arises, a feeling which he projects upon you as "You are trying to trap me." Dread of losing himself in the one who loves him involves a terrible ambivalence. He feels that he is being pulled apart by two equally powerful urges, each containing both a plus and a minus: he can approach and be loved, yet live in fear of abandonment; or he can withdraw and be "safe," yet alone.

He is extremely frightened of being nurtured, of turning into an emotional baby. He needs an unthreatening arrangement which, like Goldilocks's porridge, is neither too hot nor too cold. He doesn't believe that simultaneous belonging and independence are possible. When he is tempted to merge, he views himself as a helpless, impotent infant, the butt of men's teasing. (Men may joke about "the ball and chain," celebrate bridegrooms' last night of "freedom," speak of their women as "the boss"—but there is distress beneath the surface of the jesting.) So long as the Co-independent is trapped in this dilemma, he is never free and he never finds himself, both of which he claims as primary goals.

The Co-independent and affairs

The Co-independent may be propelled into affairs to keep himself from depending upon you. He mistakenly believes that sexual affairs will satisfy his need to belong with no strings attached. (Nonetheless, he may not care for the other woman as he cares for you.) He searches for closeness without the price of being known in a real relationship, without the cost of commitment: he wants to win the trophy without playing the game. Sex seems the obvious, magical way to achieve contact without becoming overwhelmed.

A Co-independent who roams sexually is likely at any given time to be cultivating several affairs in different stages of development. His habit of keeping even innocent comings and goings under cover makes it easier for him to hide affairs.

THE SWEETHEART

Overview

The Sweetheart's major fear is of being abandoned by you. Thus, the Sweetheart does his best to please you: he praises you, lavishes gifts upon you, is romantic and attentive. He tends to be passive, even docile. Whatever you do, he never criticizes. (You may wish he would argue with you or show that he has a mind of his own.) He is quiet and thoughtful—never flamboyant—and often smiles gently and nods in an understanding way. The Sweetheart's sincere empathy may afford him a finely tuned sensitivity to your feelings.

44

He presents himself as a gentleman, a decent sort, and is actually highly ethical in most areas. While your friends tell you how wonderful he is and how lucky you are, and although you feel well taken care of, you do not feel chal-lenged by or particularly excited about the Sweetheart. You may feel that he needs you too much and follows you too closely, like an eager puppy. If you express a desire to break up, he seems stunned and miserable, repeatedly tell-ing you how much you mean to him.

What he does and how you feel

Craving your approval—and fearing your rejection—the Sweetheart is uncomfortable with conflict. If there is a choice to be made—which restaurant, which movie, which vacation spot—he defers to you, saying, "What-ever you like will be fine with me." He claims that he has no negative thoughts about you, and when you bring up a source of tension between you, he says, "You are right," and ends it at that.

He wants you to dress conservatively to avoid attract-ing attention from other males because he's afraid of los-ing you. While he never directly disapproves of what you wear, he may encourage you to keep a bit of weight you want to lose, or to be "natural," meaning no makeup.

When you have a problem, he says, "It's all right. I'll take care of it," as if to do so is a pleasure. If he *can't* solve all your problems, he sees himself as a failure. Thus, when at a loss for an immediate solution to a difficulty with which you present him, the Sweetheart avoids the is-sue by saying, "I'll think it over," never returning to the subject.

He may be incurably optimistic, even in the face of disaster. As one woman described her man, "If we had just been hit by a nuclear bomb, he would be making funny faces in the window to cheer me up." Wanting to put the best face upon his behavior, you may conclude

45

that he is strong and calm, whereas he is actually numbed to his own emotional reactions.

He simulates intimate conversation by telling emotional stories about his childhood. Although they sound meaningful, these tales are safe to tell because they don't directly involve you. While men do need to talk about childhood issues, the Sweetheart becomes stuck in this mode because it is not so threatening as facing current feelings.

He wants you to cling to him, although he may come to feel suffocated after a time. (You too may feel suffocated by his enveloping attention.) Furthermore, because straightforward assertiveness is not part of his repertoire, his anger eventually seeps out in the form of passive-aggressive behavior: forgetting important things you may have told him; arriving late to meet you or standing you up entirely; or delaying on delivery of what he promises.

As his very sweetness permits his rage to build, he may begin to withdraw and sulk. Believing that in order to avoid rejection he cannot express his honest feelings, he comes to resent you because—according to his perception—you are forcing him to be phony. Sensing his inauthenticity, you feel similarly prohibited from expressing your feelings or revealing your own flaws.

You may be satisfied with his sweetness, or you may feel that he is somehow *too* sugary. In either case, he is consistent and certainly easy to get along with, so you may accept this superficial relationship. Because he is so fearful of "rocking the boat"—and because you are aware of his fragility—you, too, hesitate to disturb the equilibrium.

Beneath the Mask

The mask of the Sweetheart covers the face of a genuinely tender, vulnerable, often naively innocent man. The Sweetheart yearns for belonging; in fact, he is nearly obsessed with it. He needs affirmation of his character, recognition for his patience and kindness, and fears your criticism.

His mask is formed by his compulsion to avoid what he fears most—rejection. (This overriding directive leaves him little room to try to please himself or even consider his own desires.) Beneath his mask, he is panicked by the thought of not having his basic needs met. He worries that alone he could not survive, that there would be nothing left of him.

Any expressions of anger, yours or his, frighten the Sweetheart. This fear often prevents him from even the private, internal recognition of the anger that builds within him. When his cumulative rage does penetrate his awareness, he is suffused with guilt, which may drive him to turn his anger inward upon himself. The Sweetheart's dynamic can thus become the basis for depression.

The Sweetheart and affairs

A straying Sweetheart's desperate fear of rejection may lead him to find an additional partner as an "insurance policy." His affairs are likely to be long-term because they would not otherwise provide an adequate backup system. Since the Sweetheart's primary need is belonging, not sex, a married Sweetheart may have an "affair of the heart," a romance with no sex involved. Since he has always seemed so devoted, the revelation of a Sweetheart's affair is a shock to his primary partner and to others.

Because he cannot confront his resentment in a forthright manner, infidelity can also become the Sweetheart's means of expressing anger toward you. He can be surprisingly careless about leaving a trail for you to discover so that his anger is communicated. Nonetheless, because of his inherent tenderness, he may be genuinely sorry that you are hurt when you discover his infidelity.

The Dreamer

Overview

The Dreamer's major fear is of his own inadequacy. He compensates with a fantasy self-image, requiring an equally fantastic partner to support it. Thus, the exaggerated praise he showers upon you at the outset of your relationship seems unrealistic to you. Although his adoring remarks are actually sincere (arising from a fantasy image of you that he holds to be real), at times you may think he's "coming on" to you with the proverbial line. While you reason that he couldn't possibly know you as well as he appears to think he does, his adulation nonetheless can be a heady ride.

Later he is stunned when your flaws, no matter how minor, show through. For him, your faults become disillusionments instead of normal human failings, which can be accepted or overlooked. It's now your turn to be stunned: you have become accustomed to the role of the idolized one who could do no wrong.

Unlike the Co-independent, who flees when the relationship is at its best, the Dreamer tends to take flight at the first sign of trouble.

What he does and how you feel

The Dreamer's fantasy world interferes with any realistic connection with you. He is a particularly poor listener, who sometimes seems to "space out" or be "lost in a fog." Often when you talk, you don't feel that he hears what you are saying, even though he may be gazing fixedly at you. When you ask a question, he smiles instead of answering. He may astound you by forgetting something which is an essential, obvious part of your life or personality.

He prefers that you be quiet because he doesn't want you to disrupt his dreamworld by revealing your inner self or relating to him as he actually is. Rather, he wants you to remain an imaginary figure relating to his fantasy of himself. Only with someone he doesn't really know can he continue to live in his illusion.

The Dreamer effectively puts a mask of *his* choosing upon *your* face, and you must struggle to live up to this impossible image. For instance, you may play along when he wants you to dress in a manner consistent with his fantasy even though the clothes in question may make you feel silly or brazen. He may go so far as to try to dictate what you wear, especially in private, buying you sexy lingerie (perhaps failing to notice that it doesn't fit). Or he may urge you to change your hair color.

When you express a need for change in the relationship, the Dreamer seems forlorn, saying, "I thought this was the way you wanted things to be," or "I thought you really loved me." Feeling sorry for him and vaguely guilty, you may revert to trying to be "perfect" according to his distorted image of you.

He may start to become agitated or sullen when you reveal trivial frailties or discuss a problem. He seems angry when you are sick or when you are tired and neglect to put on your makeup. To you, these behaviors seem inordinately picky, and you eventually become less and less secure as you realize that you really don't fit his dream picture.

No one falls farther or harder than the partner of a Dreamer when his bubble finally bursts. When knowledge of you as a living, breathing person pierces his fantasy, he may choose to relinquish *you* instead of his illusion. He may not outwardly break away; you may only perceive in his touch, in his eyes, that he has retreated to a distant somewhere. Or he may simply disappear without leaving a trace.

Beneath the Mask

The Dreamer constructs his own world and fears being torn from it. The disruption of his fantasy would require him to face what he perceives himself to be: unworthy, incompetent, and weak, and thereby doomed to rejection. He believes he is not strong enough, competent enough, sexy and virile enough, to handle reality—including a real woman.

He may suffer from deeply entrenched, radically unrealistic childhood conditioning as to how he *should be,* and thus becomes this "should-be" person in his fantasy, to avoid being overcome by guilt and shame. This false self-image becomes the axis around which his whole world rotates, to the point that he requires a certain kind of pretend-partner to feed, support, and reflect it.

You need not think his fantasizing is a rejection of you. He does not construct daydream images because he sees *you* as inadequate, but because he sees *himself* as inferior. The fervency of his attachment to this image suggests the enormity of the pain it hides. His retreat into fantasy betrays his negative perception of himself.

The Dreamer and affairs

Since the Dreamer needs a stranger as a partner in order to maintain his masquerade, an affair may be imminent when you begin to appear to him as a real person with real faults—or even values—of your own. As he did with you in the beginning, he will avoid confronting any shadow of truth about the other woman's flawed humanity. The less he knows her, the easier it is to maintain his imaginary portrait of her . . . and of himself. As her genuine self inevitably emerges, he is likely to avoid responsibility by telling himself that *she* had represented herself to him falsely.

Since fresh partners are almost always available to the man who searches, the Dreamer can simply start over with someone else when one woman becomes too "real." He is thus cut out for short-term affairs. A series of partners preserves his fantasy and provides a measure of security. If he plays the field, then his supply of dream women cannot be withdrawn by one woman's whim, a twist of fate, or his own misdoings. He will not be without *someone,* and almost any "someone" can serve for a time as a canvas onto which the Dreamer can paint his fantasies.

THE HERO

Overview

The Hero's major fear is of not being affirmed by other men. In order to win the approval of his male peers, he conforms closely to the stereotype of the activity-oriented, take-charge man. In his view, conversation is for problem-solving, and his job is to be the "fixer." He plays the role of "the strong, silent type": when you talk, he nods or says, "Mm-mm," maintaining a silence which he believes makes him appear wise—while you may feel that he simply isn't listening. If you bring up a problem in your relationship, he may claim that there is no point in being upset, cutting you off with a remark such as, "I've learned to close such things off and not think about them." In saying this, he seems to imply that you should do the same.

What he does and how you feel

The Hero's life centers around being recognized by other men as "all man." His efforts to impress his peers range from job status and fancy cars to appearing with a stereotypically sexy-looking woman. He may take on too many activities and too much responsibility in order to fulfill what he perceives as his proper role. As a result, he is often "too busy to talk": he will talk later, he says, after this project is completed or that conflict is resolved. You may feel that you are a low priority on his list.

Recognizing that you are more skilled at talking about feelings than he is, he may fear being verbally stampeded

51

by you. When you bring up a personal matter which he does not want to discuss, he may kiss you to keep you quiet. "Let's make love," he says sweetly. If you don't go along, he wonders aloud how you can insist upon talking when you obviously don't love him. Another strategy he may adopt when you try to engage him in feeling-talk is to filibuster, telling long stories, which seem to you to have no relevance to the topic at hand.

He may be the particular brand of Hero I call Executive Man. Executive Man *does* talk—about current events, work, sports scores, and other typical "man-talk" subjects. If you say you'd like to talk about something else, he asks in genuine bewilderment: "What else is there to talk about?" Executive Man may complain that you don't want to talk about anything "really important," by which he means broad issues which are not directly personal.

Executive Man is accustomed to speaking in terms of logic, power, and ability. If the two of you are married with children, he may bring home his business *persona* and conduct family conversations like staff meetings or military conferences. He sees talking as a form of competition, like most of the activities in which he engages, and he doesn't want to lose.

The Hero may want you to wear alluring clothing in public so that other men will envy him. Even if you feel that the garments he buys you are tasteless and cheap, you may wear what he wants on certain occasions, only to have your feelings hurt when he openly gazes at other women. His rationalization: "All men look."

The Hero's emotional response is often delayed. He was taught not to have feelings and it almost worked—he doesn't react immediately. Feelings just seep through after a while. As a consequence of this time lag, you may not know why he is behaving angrily toward you when he may have appeared entirely content during your last interaction only a short time before. Unable to discern cause-

and-effect in his behavior, you may become increasingly anxious.

Beneath the Mask

The Hero is usually less fear-driven than the other masked men we have discussed. He dons his mask less to hide fear than to follow the pattern set for him as a male by American culture. The Hero mask is thus more a response to external pressures than internal psychological forces. Most Heroes are simply trying to conform to society's glorified portrait of the hero: always brave, strong, tough, unsentimental, self-sufficient, and independent.

His attempt to live up to this unattainable image brings with it its own set of fears and insecurities. If the Hero fears anything, it is falling short of the masculine cultural stereotype. (This anxiety suggests that, underneath, a Hero can be insecure in his identity as a man.) Appearing sentimental, tender, or in any other way unlike a "real man" would leave him vulnerable to the ridicule of his companions. He may dread humiliation, worry about appearing incompetent, or experience apprehension in situations where he cannot perfectly fulfill the impossible *machismo* role.

Because anger is practically the only emotion acceptable to the Hero, he tends to put the face of anger on his other highly charged feelings, such as fear and grief. Consequently, he may often appear to be inappropriately angry.

The task of keeping tight control over his emotions will be easier for the Hero if you too remain cool and collected. Thus he may exert pressure on you to keep *your* feelings contained as well.

The Hero and affairs

The Hero may have affairs at least in part to establish his masculinity and win the admiration and envy of other men. Their reinforcement encourages him to act out his instincts in this fashion without pondering the consequences.

If you confront the Hero about an affair, he is likely to say, "All guys do it. It doesn't mean anything. It's just the way we are." This is an honest response, since affairs often do not mean very much to the Hero; he usually doesn't become emotionally involved. Deep down he may really love his primary partner.

THE DEFENDER

Overview

The Defender's major fear is of your power—for which he compensates by attempting to appear as an immovable pillar of strength. In the face of emotionally challenging events, he says, with a tightening of his jaw, "I can handle it. I'm tough." He rarely smiles; he is inscrutable. You may watch his expressions vigilantly, relaxing only when his face seems serene. Proud of his hardness—equating it with strength—he may laugh, as young boys do, during a sentimental or tender scene in a play or film.

He is incurably pessimistic; in his view, people can't change, and *he* in particular can't change. "I've always been this way," he says. As far as he is concerned, such a comment terminates any dialogue you may initiate about your relationship. He says he doesn't need to talk about feelings because he is so self-sufficient: "I'm not a baby; I don't need help."

A perceptive friend may find him attractive or amusing, but tells you she's glad that *she* is not the one who is in love with him.

What he does and how you feel

The Defender may criticize your clothing, your hair, your makeup, almost never commenting favorably on

your appearance. If you ask how he likes a particular outfit, he says, "I would tell you if I didn't." And you cannot
understand why he makes comments like, "I see you've
gained a little weight."

Like little boys who form secret clubs even when they
have no secrets, the Defender needs a secret self for
security. He refuses to tell you ordinary details that would
be neither incriminating nor hurtful—because information gives you power.

He thus appears frightened when you seem to understand him, but nonetheless becomes angry when you
don't (even if to do so would require mind-reading, a skill
he appears to believe you possess). He wants you to understand, but not too much. This dilemma leaves you little room in which to maneuver safely.

The Defender hates tears. If you mention that you
need to talk, he says, "There is no point in talking. You
will just cry, and I despise emotional scenes." If the two of
you are talking and your tears start to flow, he brings the
conversation to an abrupt end.

Just as he maintains tight control over his own emotions, he must control you as well. He assumes the authority to tell you how things are, what is right and
wrong: "You spend too much time with your sister—she
just takes advantage of you." The Defender attempts to
monopolize the decision-making in your relationship,
finding fault when you take even minor initiatives: "You
paid too much for your massage—I know someone who
charges less"; "You planted the wrong kind of flowers—
they don't do well in this climate." You find yourself
capitulating, convincing yourself that such issues are too
insignificant to fight over.

Beneath the Mask

Since the Defender's motivating fear is of being ma-
nipulated by a woman, he is desperate to defend himself

from your power, to prevent himself from falling under your spell. He is terrified also of abandonment—the possibility of which grants a woman much of her power. He therefore never exposes his true self in a relationship, denying you the opportunity to reject him, at least as he really is.

If you are unpredictable, if you surprise him in any way, he is uncomfortable. The expression of your power that makes the Defender most uncomfortable—and that he will therefore tolerate the least—is your anger. In a column in *New Woman* magazine, psychiatrist Frank Pittman describes this basic male fear, so greatly exaggerated in the psyche of the Defender: "Among the most universal of male phobias is the fear of female anger . . . Men view angry women as terrifyingly powerful; their anger feels like the wrath of the gods."

As the Hero competes with other men, the Defender competes and struggles with you. He is afraid that you will overpower him: therefore, he must overpower you. Like the Hero, the Defender has an amplified need to be accepted by other men as "a real man"—but his path is through the conquest of "woman."

The Defender tends to see life in all-or-nothing, either/or terms. Entertaining no expanded alternatives, he is suspicious of concepts such as balance, equality, cooperation, and shared responsibility. He believes that in your relationship only one of two extreme situations is possible: either you dominate or he dominates. He cannot relax his guard.

His fear is pervasive. The Defender is the most wary and shielded of all masked men, the most frustrating to deal with. Whatever fears men commonly have, he has to extremes. He fears bonding. He fears rejection. He fears scenes. He fears your emotions, and is petrified of his own. He fears his own fear, for which he compensates by appearing fearless. The greater his fear, the more tenacious his masquerade.

Ever alert to any glimmer of what might lie beneath his steely mask, you may occasionally catch glimpses of his childlike vulnerability, which is precisely what the Defender is defending.

The Defender and affairs

Just as he needs promotions or victory at games or any other competition in life, the Defender sometimes has affairs in order to "win." He sees having sex with a woman as conquering her; being afraid of women, he gets a chance to enhance his feeling of power. Frank Pittman's comments on men who have many affairs are particularly relevant to the Defender: "Philanderers . . . are afraid of women . . . see them as dangerous sex objects who can give . . . masculinity as well as take it away." Affairs thus provide the Defender with a way to triumph over his fear of women and affirm his maleness at the same time.

He is particularly likely to choose women who already have high-status partners. Such a target gives the Defender an opportunity to defeat through sexual competition not only the woman, but another formidable male. As Carol Botwin says of such affairs, "The name of the game is not the woman in question but the man." Thus at times a Defender's affair may be largely an expression of ongoing competition with other men.

In closing this chapter, I would caution you once again not to classify your man as one or the other "type." The masks are not types; rather, they are intended to show you possible patterns which your partner may sometimes reveal to some degree. These descriptions are intended to enhance your understanding of your man; labeling him will only hinder the process of opening up intimate dialogue.

And before you initiate this intricate process, you need to acquire yet one more layer of understanding. Now that you have recognized your man's masks and the feelings they may cover, you can begin to explore more deeply the reasons he came to need his masks to begin with so that you may show him a new way of filling his needs, and thereby of removing his mask. The social and psychological pressures which taught him as a growing boy and young adult to conceal his authentic nature are the subjects of the next chapter. Because understanding promotes compassion, which in turn facilitates communication, the insights offered in the next chapter will help to equip you more fully for the journey ahead.

CHAPTER 3

Big Boys Don't Cry

How He Learned to Hide His Feelings

We are told that the social gap between the sexes is narrowing, but I [have] experienced life in both roles . . . [and] there seems to me no aspect of existence, no moment of the day, no contact, no arrangement, no response, which is not different for men and for women. The very tone of voice in which I [am] now addressed, the very posture of the person next [to me is different].

Jan Morris (travel writer,
male-to-female transsexual), *Conundrum*

The longing for interpersonal intimacy stays with every human being from infancy throughout life; and there is no human being who is not threatened by its loss.

Frieda Fromm-Reichmann

NOW THAT YOU HAVE a better understanding of *how* your partner masks his feelings—feelings as intense as your own—the stage is set for you to learn more about *why* he came to hide them in the first place. In this chapter we will examine how a boy's sense of *what he is* conflicts with *what he is taught to be*, and how this inner dissonance contributes to the adult male's reticence to express emotion verbally.

Reaching back in time to the beginnings of your man's masquerade will help you to cultivate the compassion necessary to bypass his defenses and encourage his freedom to *be* himself—and thus to *express* himself. When your partner realizes that he can be authentic, fulfilled, and even safer than before, *he will find the words.*

Pressures to be phony compel all of us, male and female alike: we are socialized to comply with stereotypical expectations, not to discover who we really are. For a male child, this pressure can be especially intense. It is as if he is handed his lines in a life-long play at the very moment of his birth. Forever thereafter he must perform according to the script or be permanently exiled from the stage; the stereotypical male role permits little *ad lib.*

The conditioning which interferes with many men's ability to communicate about feelings falls into two categories: social/cultural and familial/psychological. This chapter will focus first on forces of socialization to which American boys are subjected more or less universally. Taking a chronological approach that examines the cultural pressures upon boys at different stages of development, we will look at how they are conditioned differently from girls, and at the effect boys' play has upon their psyches. We will then look at psychological or familial influences, which vary more from individual to individual. Various family styles will be described as the foundations for faulty patterns of communication.

Before beginning this journey, however, we will take a brief look at its starting point. What we know about the differences between the inborn or genetic abilities and predispositions of men and women suggests that we are far more alike than different. At the end of the chapter we will see that both this original commonality, and the process of conditioning that tends to obscure it, have important implications for a man's freedom to be real, to be himself.

The Starting Point:
What Men and Women Are Born With

Males and females have most human characteristics in common. In a classic and thorough survey of the literature on gender differences, psychology researchers Eleanor Maccoby and Carol Jacklin conclude that males are probably born with higher capacities for aggressiveness and for visual-spatial and mathematical—in contrast to girls' verbal—skills. If women do, in fact, have a greater natural facility for words, some men—instinctively sensing their disadvantage and being honed to competitiveness by social pressures—may tend toward emotional silence with their mates out of reluctance to "lose" the game of verbal exchange to women. However, in terms of psychology, perception, and behavior (as opposed to physiology), these few characteristics represent the entire extent of the probable genetic differences between men and women.

Even in those masculine traits which may be genetically defined, men place at varying points along a continuum: for instance, some men are more aggressive than others. Furthermore, there is overlap between genders: the most aggressive females are more aggressive than the least aggressive males.

Significantly, emotion has *not* been identified as an arena of genetic disparity. Aside from society's role expectations, there are not female emotions and male emotions. We can safely assume that, in terms of genetic makeup, men are as vulnerable, tender, and capable of being hurt as women. Even though we tend to think of this trait as inherently feminine, females are *assigned* the role of being emotional.

Given the basic genetic similarity between male and female infants, how can we account for the vast differences we see between men and women as adults, or even

---

Myth

Tradition has it that females are inherently more emotional and more vulnerable than males, who are calmer and cooler.

Consequence

Experiencing emotions early in life, men learn to deny and repress them in order to conform to traditional social expectations. We women believe they are less emotional than we are and treat our men as though they are invulnerable. We may think there is no point in encouraging them to be open.

Reality

Psychological case studies, genetic indicators, social and cross-cultural evidence, and incidence of emotional problems, all show that men are *at least* as emotional as women, *at least as* vulnerable as women.

---

as young children? Part of the answer is that our culture initiates a kind of self-fulfilling prophecy by amplifying those gender differences that may be inborn. For example, where there may be a natural inclination for boys to be more aggressive than girls, society tends through expectations and teaching to support and intensify aggressiveness in males while diminishing it in females.

Furthermore, as mentioned earlier, society teaches males to define themselves in terms of their *differences* from women. Males are taught right from the beginning that to be truly masculine they must be totally nonfeminine. Anything girls do, boys are encouraged to avoid— and talking a lot is one of those things. "You're just like a girl" and "Don't be a sissy!" are epithets hurled at boys who choose to paint pictures, play violins, or sew. Boys are thus not allowed the freedom to experiment with different activities to discover their own preferences and aptitudes.

Boys are prohibited through this encouragement of

"difference" not only from uttering tender words but from displaying tender behaviors. If a girl plays with younger children, she is thought to be nurturing, a "little mother," whereas if a boy does the same, he may be considered "maladjusted." Men have to guard against touching other men for fear of being labeled homosexual, against touching women except those closest to them for fear of being accused of sexual aggression, and against touching children for fear of being suspected of molestation.

Although they have few inherent psychological differences, men grow up thinking they must be as different as possible from females. Being totally different in every way is something they can't achieve; therefore, they begin to wear masks, visible evidence of what they think is acceptable. If you know you are a pretender, you certainly don't want to tell someone about the real you. So injunctions concerning aggressiveness and tenderness influence men's minimal verbalization of feelings.

In *My Fair Lady,* Professor Higgins asks, "Why can't a woman be more like a man?" Women often wonder, "Why can't a man be more like a woman—and bare his feelings?" The answer lies, at least in part, in the fact that there is no comparison between the penalties suffered by boys who cross the gender divide—who are usually disparaged as "sissies"—and the relatively benign consequences for most girls—who may even gain approval as "tomboys."

Infancy and Early Childhood

From the time of a baby's birth, the treatment it receives from its parents is determined in part by their enculturated sense of what boys and girls are. There are even differences in how parents talk to male infants as opposed to females: researchers have observed that both mothers and fathers speak more often to newborn girls than to newborn boys.

Not only do parents *treat* male and female infants differently; they also *perceive* and *interpret* babies' behavior according to gender role expectations. For example, research shows that although there are no clear indications of whether a crying baby is experiencing fear or fury, parents more often perceive baby boys as enraged and baby girls as afraid. Parents then respond to the emotion they expect. Such perceptions influence the baby's development.

This kind of conditioning continues into adulthood. Grown men and women can perceive parallel feelings in totally different terms, labeling their responses according to stereotype. For instance, Dr. Virginia O'Leary placed a group of male and female adults in situations designed to provoke emotional reactions. While measurements of physiological arousal were identical in both sexes, the men tended to report feelings of anger at the very moments that women experienced sadness. Each gender interpreted the same physical reaction in their separate, socially acceptable ways.

Preschoolers learn their gender roles through modeling and through reward and punishment. They watch their mothers and fathers, big brothers and sisters, and copy their behaviors. They emulate playmates who seem to be reaping the rewards of "doing it right." Smiles and frowns, smacks and deprivations, ice-cream cones and bedtime stories are given for success or failure in maintaining the prescribed role. The major reinforcement for the boychild under six is getting or not getting what he needs most—acceptance from his parents. The father who comforts his little daughter when she cries may answer his son's tears with a stern look or shaming words: "Big boys don't cry." The message is: don't express your feelings.

Even while anger is somewhat encouraged as an emotional outlet for males and aggressiveness is considered a desirable masculine trait, the extent of natural, normal male aggressive fantasy may exceed the bounds of what is culturally acceptable. Research has shown that, as early as the age of two, boys' fantasies are more aggressive than girls'—possibly reflecting an inborn tendency. Girls are far less likely to be preoccupied with revenge, aggression, or sexual thoughts. They tend to fantasize in more socially approved modes: their mental pictures of romantic scenes are not generally objectionable to adults as boys' specific sexual and aggressive imaginings can be.

Thus, from early childhood on, a boy's inner life tends more often to meet with disapproval than a girl's. A boy is forced to keep his fantasies more carefully hidden than a girl is, not because he feels less, but because he has overpoweringly *strong feelings.*

And because so many of his thoughts and feelings are often forbidden by those who significantly shape his life, a boy's inner world can become a threat *to him.* His ripening conscience tells him that some of his thoughts are "bad," and his shame keeps him silent.

This concealment makes the images all the more menacing, like the monster glimpsed in the shadows that might be seen as a dustmop in the light of day. Buried feelings expand, and while verbalizing can illumine the dark corners of the mind and break this cycle, the male is typically forbidden to talk. Thus the process of repression begins.

Little boys are not born with the inclination to bear all pain impassively. Not only do American boys learn very early not to cry, *they learn to pretend they don't want to!* They are not just shamed for showing suffering, something much more injurious happens: they are pressed not to *have* such feelings. Real feelings are suffocated by the incessant portrayal of "tough, cool guy."

And, in a warped way, it works. Psychology researchers Beth Moore and Dwight Havercamp have found that men can indeed learn "not to *experience* or *recognize* emotion." Ask a woman how she felt in a given situation and usually she will tell you. Ask a man this same question and usually he will tell what *happened,* not how he felt about it. Ask him again, more pointedly, and he may say he doesn't know, that he never thought about it.

At first the male child denies his tender, forbidden thoughts and feelings. Finally, quite apart from his awareness, the lower levels of his consciousness suck the forbidden feelings under, so that he eventually, unconsciously and automatically, represses them. At that point, he is no longer aware of his own emotion.

Middle Childhood

Differences in cultural expectations for each gender become more pronounced in middle childhood (ages six to twelve). Usually, neither the cultural nor the familial constellations offer us sufficient permission or encouragement to be what *we* want to be. The dissonance between a boy's feelings about himself and what he is permitted to say compels him to talk less as time passes.

Parents, teachers, and friends all tend to present girls with confluent—non–opposing—directives. All of these sources of gender expectations agree in general about "what little girls should be." (For women, role conflicts usually emerge later when they begin to understand how ineffectively cultural conditioning has prepared them for life.) For boys, however, early pressures are inconsistent and contradictory.

Just when he is beginning to adapt at home, a boy entering school is catapulted into the society of his peers. Attitudes and actions that have met with parental approval are rarely the same as those encouraged by other youngsters—and even a boy's mother and father may give opposing instructions. Thus, youthful male behavior is fragmented into separate spheres: that which pleases the mother, that which pleases the father, that which pleases the peer group, and that which pleases teachers.

While parents and teachers may alter a boy's behavior with appropriate rewards and punishments, such authority figures are no longer the exclusive source of approval. The growing boy now focuses on the new challenge of winning the applause of his schoolmates.

If a schoolboy defends himself physically (an act likely to win respect from his father), he won't be "picked on," but his teacher may disapprove or punish. If he doesn't conceal his gentle side (which his mother may cultivate), he doesn't "fit in" at school. While his mother or his teacher (typically a woman) may tell him that "good boys don't say naughty things," he may see that "good boys" don't have friends.

In accordance with the traditional assumption that children naturally prefer the company of same-sex peers and enjoy different recreations according to their gender, most school-age children today are still segregated for sports and extracurricular activities. Injunctions as to what is expected of them, what they should do, and how they should act are expressed in terms of gender: "nice *girls* don't throw mud," "good *boys* don't hit girls," "what a sweet *girl*," "what a strong *boy*," "listen to what she *said*," "look at what he *did*!"

Some of the disparities evident in how men and women approach verbal communication actually originate in boys' and girls' characteristic styles of play. Because openness is less risky for them, girls communicate emotion in the course of their ordinary play. They frequently pretend with dialogue, acting out parties or weddings or playing the speaking roles of bride, secretary, mother, actress, teacher, or nurse, as well as some roles which break the gender barrier, such as executive, chemist, or principal.

While girls tend to rehearse scenarios in which they might realistically be expected to participate as adults, boys more often pretend to be magical characters of action who speak few words. They play the roles of race-car drivers, "cops and robbers," cowboys, and fantasy figures. They emulate "superheroes," who embody the masculine stereotype of unrealistic, impossible power. This type of play features little verbal interchange. Boys are more likely to imitate the noises of airplanes, guns, and machinery—feelingless objects—or to yell "gotcha!" or "I won!" than to act out scenarios requiring complex dialogue. This contrast in play sets the stage for female children to enter adulthood with verbal skills that their male counterparts may lack.

It is usually only among his companions that a young boy can safely share some of the highly erotic and aggressive, forbidden feelings discussed in the previous section. His peers encourage him to exaggerate, boast, and make jokes about sex. They take him into territory even his father would forbid: genital play, smoking, life-risking adventures.

And within such a group, making fun of "girlish" feelings is typically compulsory for belonging. Isolation is the ultimate psychological punishment, and among his peers nothing is as isolating for a young boy as being labeled a "sissy." His effort to act like one of the boys may persist throughout adulthood.

Several men have told me stories about how, when they were as young as eight or nine, their fathers took them hunting. These tales, which so neatly illustrate the pressures other males exert upon boys to be "manly," typically go as follows:

At first excited to be "one of the men," the boy shoots and kills an animal and, immediately sickened, crumples into tears. Embarrassed by his son's display of emotion, the father warns his boy to "act like a man," while other men in the party tease him about being a sissy, laugh at him, or shake their heads in disgust. The youth is forced to pick himself up, shut off his feelings, and go on with the hunt. The lesson learned: to be a man, to be accepted by men, he must not be compassionate and must not show real feelings. He must be *hard*.

One man told me that he was so nauseated when he killed his first deer that he never hunted again. Yet, he said, he would soon take his son, nearing twelve, on a hunting trip because he wanted him to "fit in." This sensitive man found it necessary to betray his own convictions and probably his son's feelings, so fearful was he that his boy might be considered "different." This story serves as a poignant example of how apparently indelible the imprint of masculine enculturation can be.

As a growing boy acts out the gender role expected of him, he becomes increasingly out of touch with his real emotions, less and less likely to *feel* his fears, hurts, and vulnerabilities. Like a masterful actor who has *become* his role while on stage, the developing male may cease to wonder how *he* feels; the pressures of his role change him within as well as without.

He becomes so separated from others by the shroud of secrecy that society is weaving around his real self that no one truly knows him—and *he does not know himself.* One or another aspect of his being must remain hidden from everyone in his life. And talking, which he needs to do in order to sort out and define his feelings—and therefore himself—is precisely what he cannot do.

Adolescence

Puberty marks the point at which a boy's conformity to gender expectation becomes a "do or die" struggle. At this time in his life he is no longer a boy who is expected to act "like a man," but, at least as far as physiological maturity and bodily stature are concerned, he is becoming a man in *fact*. Lapses into "femininity" that may have been tolerated when he was younger are penalized with a new severity by his peers and male role models such as his father, his gym teacher, or his older brother.

The pressure is on. He may be expected to join a sports team, where the level of competition and physical rough and tumble can be excruciating—far more intense than it was in the games of earlier boyhood. Fistfights and scuffles with other boys (whose size and physical strength—like his own—are generally far greater than they were only a few years before) may become more than mere unpleasant incidents. These confrontations can now take on the proportions of life-threatening or at least potentially quite injurious battles; and adults, who do not necessarily continue to hold the physical upper hand over the growing youngsters, may no longer be able to intercede as effectively.

As his body undergoes rapid changes and his sexual hormones erupt tumultuously, a boy is tossed into competition of a new sort—the bewildering dating game, often less a matter of winning affection than of capturing the crucial envy and admiration of other boys. He experiences conflicting pressures in this arena: while his teachers and his parents may discourage him from pursuing his sexual impulses, his peers are likely to applaud him for collecting "hits" and "scores"—and to humiliate him mercilessly if they suspect he is sexually inexperienced.

In adolescence, a boy's relationships with females, now becoming substantively "romantic" if not literally sexual, begin to take on the patterns that will characterize his adulthood. He begins to select—perhaps unconsciously—the masks that he will wear. In this period, boys thus start to make appearances in the roles of the Co-independent, the Sweetheart, the Dreamer, the Hero, and the Defender.

It is among teenagers that being "cool"—with all that the word implies about a lack of passionate expression—

becomes paramount. An impassive demeanor is often socially reinforced within the peer group. Those few occasional expressions of tenderness and vulnerability that may have been overlooked in a boy may well vanish entirely, for now the boy must become a "real man."

How Families Inform Patterns of Communication

To a greater or lesser extent, virtually all American boys are subject to the social forces described above. These factors form an omnipresent, generalized field of pressure that pushes a growing boy further and further away from talking about—and even being aware of—his feelings.

However, this kind of conditioning (a certain amount of which is necessary for both boys and girls if they are to survive in society) can be mitigated or massively amplified by the habits, rules, and patterns surrounding communication that prevail in a particular family. Pertinent to the question of why your partner cannot disclose his feelings is the examination of how a man comes to feel unloved, ashamed, inadequate, guilty, or confused about his identity. The nature of such influences, which vary greatly from person to person, thus plays a crucial role in determining a man's individual style of communication and the selection of masks he is likely to wear.

Below are described several more or less common family patterns. Each discussion concludes with an explanation of the messages or injunctions about communication and about himself that a boy receives from his family's behaviors, along with a summary of some of the consequences that can ensue from his absorption of this programming.

As you read, perhaps you will recognize some of the psychological forces to which your man was exposed in *his* family, and thereby discover possible factors relevant to his style of communication. Keep in mind that some of these patterns are relatively severe, and therefore tend to produce men who are more troubled than is typical of "masked men"; your man may have suffered subtler versions of syndromes which for purposes of concise description are recounted here in their more extreme forms.

1. The father teaches his son to keep secrets from his mother.

The father, an action-oriented man who is rarely talkative, focuses on shared activities in his relationship with his son. As they head home with satisfaction from an adventurous day, he may caution his son, "You'd better not tell your mother; women don't understand these things," or "We won't tell anyone about this, OK?" Secret father-son activities range from daredevil pursuits like rock climbing, which Mother is likely to see as too dangerous, to eating candy bars for dinner, which she deems unhealthy.

The puzzled boy fears that if he doesn't keep quiet about his doings with Dad he may be punished or a fight may break out between his parents. He thus believes that his father is protecting him by advising him not to talk. The boy is never quite sure about what he should avoid telling, so he reveals nothing.

When father and son arrive home and Mother asks, "How did you enjoy your day?" the boy may look at his father for cues as to how to respond. His father's expressions and behavior communicate that the boy had best just remain quiet and smile. (Although he imitates his father's behavior, he can only guess what feelings underlie it.)

Message: Disclosure to a woman is dangerous; say nothing. As the boy's father said, "Women don't understand." Since Father's attitude encourages an image of women as fearfully powerful, Defenders sometimes come from such families.

2. Mother reports on her son to his father.

When the boy breaks a rule, even if he is not certain what the rule is, his mother avoids the chore of disciplining him by saying, "Wait till I tell your father." If she follows through on this threat, the father obviously becomes the one who administers the punishment, but the mother is nonetheless the one responsible for its taking place. Mother is at best vague about the nature of the penalty that Father will exact; and the delay between the boy's infraction and its consequences, which must await Father's arrival, is nervous-making. These two factors leave plenty of room for the boy's anxiety to feed itself and swell out of proportion, perhaps causing him more suffering than the punishment itself, which may not even actually occur.

Message: The more a woman knows about a man, the more opportunity she has to betray him. It is best to tell a woman nothing. Once again, the woman becomes an object of fear; Defenders may also emerge from this family pattern.

73

3. The mother always seems to know what her boy is doing.

The boy is unpleasantly surprised to discover that his mother consistently knows he's "up to something" when he is unusually quiet. He fails to realize that his very quietness, by which, he had reasoned, he would avoid attention, has been her tip-off. Thus he comes to believe that she can read his mind. One client of mine told me that when he was a child he would shut the door to his room at night because he thought his mother could see his dreams.

Message: Since a woman already knows what's on a man's mind, there is little point in communicating with her. The boy may cover up as much activity and emotion as he can in an attempt to offset the frightening power of her intuition. His hidden world may become elaborated into a complex fantasy life, a means of privacy which often produces a Dreamer.

Women can be quite intuitive and seem to know more about their mates than the men may be comfortable with. Such men may behave unpredictably (as does the Co-independent) in order to compensate for their mates' seemingly magical apprehension of their whereabouts and activities.

4. The mother speaks for the boy, tells others how he feels, what he thinks, and what he is.

For example, the boy hears his mother say to a neighbor, "My son is too shy to make friends." The boy may not feel that this is true, and indeed his mother's statement may be false. Perhaps *she* wishes him *not* to make friends because she fears influences outside of her control, and is unconsciously attempting to initiate a self-fulfilling prophecy. She may tell his teacher he was proud of his role in the school play even though he saw himself as more embarrassed than proud. In any case, she almost never asks what he wants or feels.

Message: He comes to believe, "I don't know how I feel or what I am. She knows." Since he doesn't dare contradict his mother, he lets her do the talking. He may grow up to be a Sweetheart.

5. His mother tells him how he feels.

When the boy discloses strong feelings, his mother contradicts him. If he says that he hates a certain relative, she says, "No you don't. You don't *really* hate anyone." If he is upset over an unpleasant incident, such as the loss of a favorite toy, she may invalidate him with a dismissal such as, "You're just tired."

Message: Women don't want to be confronted with a man's real feelings. Receiving no affirmation for knowing and expressing himself, a child subjected to such treatment never learns to trust his own interpretations of his feelings, and may come to believe that others can actually know him better than he knows himself. Learning to surrender his own thoughts in deference to a woman's perceptions, he may become a Sweetheart.

6. His mother enforces polite words even when they run counter to his feelings.

Mother insists that he say things he doesn't feel, that he tell a relative whom he dislikes that he is happy to see her, that he apologize to his sister for something he isn't sorry for. All expressions of feeling except the superficial are forbidden, and no one seems to care what *he* feels.

Message: Never say anything negative to or about anyone else. Even though the boy may have heard his mother speak critically of others, he feels guilty when he does so himself. He comes to believe that his feelings don't count as much as those of others. The injunction to "be phony" usually penetrates his psyche more deeply than the injunction to "be kind." Thereby coming to perceive "nice" behavior as an indication of phoniness, the boy may grow up distrusting kind words. Since males in this culture are coerced into not being too "nice," these maternal prescriptions add up once again to the overpowering message: Don't say anything at all.

7. The father cautions the boy not to cry or otherwise show physical or emotional pain.

The boy may be punished for verbalizing his feelings of hurt even if he doesn't act upon them. He has no role model for expression of genuine, tender feelings.

Message: A "real man" is insensitive. As an adult, the boy may "forget" to say the appropriate gentle word because to do so would hint at his own vulnerability. He thinks that even those who care most about him do not want to hear his real feelings. He subsequently denies that he *has* such feelings until, perhaps, he no longer does. Heroes can grow from such roots.

8. The family has secrets. They tell the boy not to say anything to anyone about them at any time.

Shame and fear go everywhere with this boy. Shame is rarely rational: certain families are deeply humiliated by, and therefore desperately hide, that which others may shrug off or even openly broadcast. Perhaps a family member is in prison, or has a communicable disease or an addiction. Some families are ashamed of a divorce, a suicide, cancer, or a mentally retarded member. In a family permeated with shame, the child feels that he too is somehow "bad."

Message: Anything you disclose can be used against you. Clients of mine often cannot imagine being able to articulate their secrets, much less being accepted after the telling. Most such secrets do not involve transgressions they have committed, but rather their own victimization by others. Yet, like a rape victim, they feel humiliated because of the offenses committed against them. Defenders are sometimes molded by this suppressive kind of family.

9. There is a secret that is not discussed even within the confines of the family.

This "elephant in the living room" syndrome revolves around an obvious issue that family members nonetheless pretend does not exist. Perhaps the parents frequently have loud arguments; the children huddle in their rooms, silently exchanging troubled glances with each other. When the conflict subsides and it seems safe to come out, the children take up their appointed places, pretending that the fight never occurred. They know that it is unacceptable to verbally acknowledge such an event.

Or perhaps the boy mentions to his mother that his father came home drunk the night before. She may turn on him angrily, shouting: "Of course he didn't! Why would you ever say such a thing?" One of my clients told me that his family was sometimes in such turmoil that no one fed the children. If he asked when he could have his dinner, he was told that he had already eaten!

Message: The child is "bad" to notice, to be aware, and especially to say so. He learns not to trust his own perceptions, much less to express them. It is best to act as if "everything's just fine." In a sense, a problem becomes real only when you talk about it. Such denial can produce Heroes.

10. The family rarely talks about anything.

The parents go about their business in almost total silence. Mother takes care of the child, more or less, touching him only occasionally and in a hollow way, not communicating with him even through smiles or eye contact. Father comes home, sits down at the table, and eats without a word. In this family, conversation has no function other than the transfer of essential information.

Adult children from such families might report that after a significant family event such as the death of a sibling: "My parents said *nothing*. I just realized my brother was not there and all the grown-ups looked upset. Then we went to the funeral. It was only then that I knew for sure."

Message: Don't talk at all. The only option left may be to act out emotions instead. (It is the supercontrolled who finally act out dramatically.) Longing for the love their parents did not express, but having learned only how to be emotionally distant, boys from such families may develop the confusing ambivalence of the Co-independent.

11. The parents project guilt upon the boy.

Fault is consistently laid upon the boy even in regard to events for which he could not possibly have been responsible. For example, if his mother falls down the stairs while he is outside playing, he is blamed. Her clumsiness, she claims, was because she was distracted with worry over where her son was. Being held responsible for incidents that take place even when he isn't present, he may begin to falsify his whereabouts to better justify his absences. For instance, he maintains that he was late for dinner not because he was playing baseball, but because he was studying with a friend.

He may hear his parents quarreling about him, and, if they subsequently separate, feel that he is responsible. His mother may warn him not to irritate his father, so that, if his father abuses her, the boy somehow feels that he should have been able to prevent it.

Message: In order to avoid blame, you must lie to others; in order to avoid guilt, you must lie to yourself. Lying may become compulsive for a boy raised in such a family. As an adult, he may constantly pretend that he was not where he was, was not doing what he was doing, and ultimately that he is not who he is. He will say he was working when actually he has been playing. And, finally, he may not know the truth at all. Out of touch with his feelings, the boy grows into a Dreamer.

78

12. The boy's parents threaten him with utter rejection.

If he expresses his own thoughts or feelings—such as articulating his fury about a decision his parents made concerning him—the boy is told, "We won't love you anymore if you don't stop talking like that." Parents following more extreme patterns of this kind may even blackmail him with total abandonment, threatening to send him away to a foster home or put him up for adoption. There may be no consistency: the boy may be punished for saying something which his parents earlier smiled at. He can thus form no clear definition of those behaviors which constitute the crossing of the invisible line. He may watch his parents uneasily, trying to get a sense of their mood in an attempt to discern whether he has violated their imperceptible limits.

Message: Because he was regularly condemned for saying

how he felt, and since he cannot predict which verbal expressions might provoke devastating rejection, the boy learns to keep quiet, keep his face blank, and keep his inner self invisible. This family pattern may produce the Sweetheart, who compensates for abandonment fear with exaggerated compliance, or the Co-independent, who prevents his own rejection by rejecting his partner *first.*

Because of a child's absolute dependence upon his parents, the threat of abandonment is tantamount to the threat of death. A connection is made in the boy's unconscious mind between disclosure and annihilation.

Can He Change His Past?

We—men and women alike—collectively participate in maintaining the *status quo.* Women tend to think, "That's just how men are," meaning that a man's temperament is part of his nature and nothing can be done about it. She responds to him as if that were true. Some men may affirm this belief, saying, "That's just how I am."

However, as the explorations in this and previous chapters indicate, the kind of emotional silence which we see as "typically male" is largely a learned characteristic. It is possible to unlearn and relearn, to rise above our societally imposed responses.

The feminist revolution provides evidence that we can break away from a cultural emphasis on narrow gender roles. Traditionally, women have been conditioned into docile modes. However, only recently have we come to a collective realization that traits, such as passivity, which we originally considered to be female nature, were actually dependent upon cultural training. With feminist consciousness-raising we have now discovered that we have been shaped by society, and that we can act in the direction of change. Although the transformation has been slow, there is no doubt that women in the United States exhibit different behaviors, and even have different feelings, than did women thirty years ago.

And today we can see the beginnings of a "masculinist" movement, a sense of awakening stimulated and supported by writers such as groundbreaker Warren Farrell, Robert Bly, who wrote *Iron John,* and Sam Keen, author of the men's bestseller *Fire in the Belly.* These books, and the movement they inform and reflect, encourage men to cast off cultural stereotypes and to become more aware of their emotion as a healthy, natural, even desirable part of their being.

People—men as well as women—*can* change. Even that which is *nature* can be significantly modified. It *is* possible to overcome natural tendencies which work against us. At the beginning of this chapter we reviewed a few differences between men and women that are possibly inborn, among these a higher capacity for verbal skills in women. However great or small may be the magnitude of an inborn trait's influence on the issues of gender communication, it in no way represents an intractable barrier. Such inherent characteristics are everywhere amended in various directions by different cultures and by the individuals who shape our development.

Our instinctive drives push us to engage in sex whenever and with whomever we wish, or to hurt those who frustrate our needs and desires. Nonetheless, most of us control such impulses. We restrain our natural urges, except under more or less socially approved circumstances. The energy firing our instinctive aggressions can be sublimated and channeled into productive, constructive action.

The famous anthropologist Margaret Mead and others have described a handful of small societies which, in the absence of predators and enemies, have *not* molded men and women into the roles traditional to our culture. Certain attributes (the urge to compete is a fine example) which we consider natural have not been developed in certain other cultures. Mead observed one island group,

the Arapesh, which does not differentiate males and females on the basis of temperamental traits (for instance,
the attribution of peacefulness to women and bravery to
men). Among the Arapesh, there are not "good men" and
"good women," but simply "good *people,*" and the stan-
dards by which one is deemed "good" are the same for
both genders. Gentleness is a virtue for men and for
women. Couples engage in tender sex play, with no ag-
gressor or submissive partner. Men and women treat both
male and female infants alike—with tenderness.

This chapter has shown something of how men are
shaped to silence about their emotions. Breaking out of
cultural conformity requires energy and insight, as well as
a brave heart—on your part and on his. *Because male and
female roles are born of interactions and played out in interactions, they can be changed only through interactions.* Therefore,
your participation is vital. You cannot reasonably expect
that your man will change alone.

Short of cultural revolution (or evolution), the only
way for an individual male to shed this heavy defensive
coat is to begin to talk. The critical handicap here is that
the emotions he most needs to talk about are exactly those
he has been taught to keep secret. The deception itself
binds him in; the more material he is hiding, the more
frightened he becomes of expressing *any* feeling.

Until men are liberated from the constraints of their
acculturation, you must be to your man what feminism
has been to women—a source of permission and inspira-
tion to come out from behind his wall and become real.
With your deepened understanding, you can now begin a
process of unlearning and relearning that will open doors
for you both. Regardless of the obvious advantages for
both of you, you cannot *force* your man to talk. What you
can do is *liberate* him from restraints that prevent his disclosure—*give him the safety to be himself.* That is the subject
of chapter four.

🔊

CHAPTER 4

Connecting

How to Cultivate an
Atmosphere of Trust

. . . by listening with her heart, she was able to understand something deeper than the words.
W. D. Witherall, *Chekhov's Sister*

NOW THAT YOU HAVE deepened your understanding of your man's barriers to intimate talk, the next step toward emotional disclosure is to establish the kind of setting and context in which feelings can flow. This chapter offers ideas for creating an atmosphere that encourages the sense of emotional safety your partner needs in order to freely experience and reveal his feelings. The pages ahead will discuss: the importance of consistently setting aside private time for verbal touch; ways of handling the anxiety that you may feel about what your partner might have to say; the skills of healing listening; the art of going behind and around—rather than directly assaulting—your partner's defenses; and the fundamental requirements for trustful dialogue.

While the decision to talk or to remain silent will always remain with your partner, your best chance at verbal intimacy comes through your own openness about your own feelings and your willingness to expose your spirit in its unshadowed state, thereby sustaining a climate of safety for your mate's disclosures.

The Importance of Private Time

As you enter into the task of changing your patterns of communication, two obstacles that must be overcome at the outset are time pressures and lack of privacy. Being alone together is a necessary element in crystallizing your efforts toward intimate dialogue. Setting aside private time to talk allows you to listen to each other attentively, to be more focused, and less distracted. As a consequence, your responses to each other will be more thoughtful and carefully considered.

Nonetheless, if your partner catches you at a busy time with a tentative, opening revelation, don't neglect this opportunity for communication. *Listen.* If the topic seems to call for further discussion, tell him that you don't feel able at that moment to give the subject the attention it deserves. Determine with him a time when the two of you can talk more about it. If his problem turns out to be urgent or of great importance, take advantage of his present mood for disclosure. Drop what you are doing as quickly as you can and shift your attention to him.

My clients say to me, "We never have time to ourselves. By the time our work is done and the kids get to bed, we are exhausted." In such instances, I suggest that they carefully examine how they spend their days. While we might think that our primary relationships are our top priority, a close look at how we actually spend each hour of the day may reveal that we put almost everything else first. Even if your relationship is most important in your mind, you may not realize that how you spend your days is how you spend your life. Life does not begin some other time.

Like a growing child, a relationship does not stop and

wait until we have time to devote to it; it continues to evolve whether or not we are paying attention. We must give present, immediate, and daily priority to what comes first.

Couples who faithfully keep their appointments with me (and pay for them!) tell me they never had *free* time to accomplish my assignment to them: to meet with each other for one hour each day. Yet if I say, "OK. Try for half an hour," that's no better. "Fifteen minutes?" It still doesn't work, because time is not the problem. Living in the future is the problem.

Alone time is essential for the process of intimate connection. If time is not scheduled in advance, you may hesitate to ask for it, postponing what you need to say, thinking it isn't that important, feeling embarrassed to make an "issue out of nothing." Even when you have no particular matter to discuss, arranging for privacy makes talking *possible.* Once good talk starts, you will celebrate having set aside time—time which becomes recreational, intimate, and life-sustaining.

When You Fear What You Will Hear

In order to enable your man to be comfortable, you must overcome your immediate fearful responses to what he might say. Just as men construct fantasy women, women envision their ideal men; we have dreams of what our lives will be like. *When such illusions are threatened, men avoid telling and women avoid hearing.* Your partner's fear of talking is easily paralleled by your fear of listening. One of the reasons men aren't comfortable telling us their feelings is that we are not always comfortable hearing them. A man's dread of exposing his real self is not entirely irrational. Your fear of knowing his feelings is reality-based, too.

In fact, dread of what your partner might reveal can cause you to unconsciously sabotage your own efforts toward intimate talk. Neither of you may want to talk, and you may, therefore, collude in pretending things aren't the way they are, just as some of the families in chapter three did.

Men do have things to say that women cringe to hear—their harem fantasies, their flirtations, their affairs (with women and sometimes other men), their fears, addictions, illegal acts, personal furies. We don't want our men to be weak, to have fears and flaws; we want them to take care of us, to be strong. We don't want them to say they are angry with us; we want them to say they love us. You don't want your mate to say he desires other women, that he has actually had sex with someone else; you want him to say you are ultimately desirable. You want him to say how crazy he is about you, not how much he resents you.

When a woman says she wants her man to talk, she generally has in mind that he become less inhibited in expressing love, tenderness, and warmth—not rage, fear, and hurt. When *his* talk triggers *your* fears, when you hear the verbalization of what you dread, you will feel like shutting off, just like the families who could make believe their reality wasn't there.

Your perception may be that you are safer if he does not say things which threaten you; actually you are safer if he does. While you may *feel* secure on a sinking ship if the music keeps playing, you *are* more secure if the sirens go off. Facing the reality of your partner's feelings might be immediately painful, but those alarm signals can enable you to rescue your relationship. Intimacy requires that each of you know the other's basic truths. If he can talk through heavy emotions, he is less likely to act them out.

What are the words about you that you dread and fear to hear him say? For most of us, the worst are:

- He is enraged with you;
- He resents you;
- He feels suffocated by you;
- He hates you;

- He is afraid of you;
- He is sick of you;
- He doesn't love you or doesn't know whether he does;
- He loves someone else or thinks he might;
- He is having or has had an affair or thinks maybe he will;
- Good-bye.

On some level, we don't so much want our men to *reveal* their feelings, as we want them to *change* their feelings. *We don't want them to feel what they do feel.* You want to select your partner's feelings—and that is not possible. Sensing this, a man will, understandably, shore up his defenses.

You either create an atmosphere for deception and evasion *or* you establish an environment for spontaneity. *You learn to hear it all or you will hear none of it.* When you think you are going to die of what you are hearing, it takes courage on your part to listen effectively. You must then have faith in the result.

If he does say frightening, hurtful things, is there hope for shaping a new relationship, one with trust and intimacy? Yes. Some of us have heard all of the above and somehow survived. It was awful, not what we anticipated if he ever started to talk. We went on, though, to create a vibrant new dance, minus masquerade.

Once he becomes free to express himself about whatever he feels, when the two of you have had a chance to talk in depth, he can begin to tell you what you'd like to hear as well because he's more likely to *feel* those loving things.

Waiting With Your Feelings

Becoming a healing listener requires waiting, absorbing, and affirming his words. In some measure, set *aside* (*don't* put down) your own emotions for a time. When your partner says what you dread, take care of yourself *inside yourself,* without immediately responding with your first feelings. Learn to call a moratorium on the *verbalization* of your own responses, *while you hear him out.* Don't pretend not to have feelings—just *temporarily* stop your own spoken responses, giving him a chance to speak and elaborate.

Let yourself continue to *feel your own feeling,* while nevertheless *hearing his feeling, being both outwardly aware*—hearing what he has to say and supporting his disclosure—and *inwardly aware*—delaying your responses until you have fully heard what your partner has to say. Then you can express your own apprehension and your longing for reassurance.

So that he will not interpret your delayed response as lack of caring, tell your partner, when you begin a heavy discussion, that you will *try to wait* with your feelings while he talks. Make a commitment to listen to all he has to bring to light. Collect yourself and say something such as, "OK. I'm prepared to hear what you have to say, even if I don't like it, because I know we can't get anywhere until I do. I know I'm going to have a lot to say if this is a big thing, but I will do my best to wait until you're finished. And I promise I won't walk out while you're talking."

How do you cope with your emotions while you hear what you fear? How do you wait, listening, without exploding? What if you are hearing words that are potentially devastating? For example, few disclosures are as threatening to a woman as her man's confession of an affair. Many things your man says may strike *one* of your fear chords, but hearing about the other woman plays your entire keyboard.

Hearing such a major revelation, you can *choose* to wait a while with your own feelings until you hear your partner out *if* you can do that without blotting out your own emotion. To listen and listen well without interrupting when what you're hearing is your worst nightmare takes enormous courage and discipline. If you are too detached, he might think you don't care. This is the tight-rope: on one side, the appearance of coldness, and on the other, major hysteria! Make your best attempt to walk *above* both extremes, with *balance.*

Still, *you have a right to fall apart if that's what you feel,* since rational discussions do not always provide the neces-sary release from rage or injury. If, for any reason, you cannot hold your emotion in limbo, if your words come flowing out on your tears or temper, go ahead and be *im-mediately real.* That's just fine; you must not become an au-tomaton. If you have to numb yourself to keep quiet even for a while, go ahead and be noisy. You can start over later and hear what remains to be said. In most circumstances, you will hear more if you listen, *then* tell, but *it is still better to express than suppress.*

Would you be running a risk by venting your feelings? Of course. There is risk in this entire process of baring feelings. I hope I have been successful in my attempt to persuade you that the risk is worthwhile.

One qualification: *If it has been your habit to keep quiet, seldom expressing your feelings, you especially need to let your-self reveal your true emotion.* Your problem is *not* how to wait while he talks but to discover when it is time to quit waiting and take the leap. In trying to please your man, or in trying not to suffer so much, you must not shut your own feelings off altogether.

Becoming a Healing Listener

Listening is an act of healing, an openness, a receptivity that creates a sense of space, of being accepted. Listening provides emotional sanctuary, allowing your partner to say what he feels, and *be* himself. Listening suggests that you trust him enough to hear him out, and that he trusts you enough to say whatever is on his mind. *Being heard is a component of being loved.*

Perfected attention—hungry listening—is, in fact, a way to live fully in the moment, a method of putting aside regret and dread and concentrating on the present. We automatically focus in this way when we meet someone new in whom we are interested, but the focus tends to blur in long-term relationships.

The healing power of listening is one of the major underpinnings of all psychodynamic therapy; the talk *is* the therapy. And you can learn the skills of focused attention that effective therapists employ.

Psychotherapists elicit clients' repressed thoughts and emotions by asking probing questions, by listening well, accepting what they hear, and supporting further disclosure. Basic psychodynamic theory supports the human need to verbalize instinctive emotions—anger, fear, hurt—while actually *feeling* the feelings as we talk.

A professional listener pays interested attention, does not change the subject or tell a client he shouldn't say what he has said. She neither judges nor breaks confidence. She thinks about the patterns of his history and encourages the articulation of his stories. These are therapeutic, healing attitudes *you* can develop.

However, there are certain attributes of professional therapy which you do want to avoid. To fake imperturbable detachment is to be like your unexpressive partner; the whole point of our process is that *both* of you have an opportunity to be authentic, getting in touch with the raw arousal of emotion. Never, ever, pretend that you don't respond intensely—that you are just a stranger, a spectator, listening in with no stake in the outcome. Then *you'll* be the one not disclosing feelings, dissociating from your real self.

We are involved with our men and have feelings of our own about what they say and do. If your partner says, "I think I'm falling in love with someone else," you'd be a robot to reply like a therapist, "Yes, tell me more about it." Such behavioral dissonance will only seal up your bitterest, most terrible feelings. At the same time, you do need to hear what he has to say. As indicated in the introduction of this book, you *can,* with practice, use some of the techniques an effective therapist uses, becoming a healing listener.

The following suggestions can enable you to become a healing listener, absorbed in the words you hear:

1. Begin to hear clearly; resensitize yourself to routine words.

If you have heard a phrase repeatedly, you may tend to ignore it; you may never have really *heard* it. Sharpen your awareness of your patterns of dialogue, the rhythm of your back-and-forth, by deliberately listening as though you have never before heard your partner.

2. Listen to yourself.

Without becoming paralyzingly self-conscious or judgmental, begin to be more aware of your own words. How closely do they correspond to what you are really trying to communicate? Do you tend to rely on the same well-worn phrases, thereby perhaps desensitizing your partner to their meanings? Do you tend to express yourself vaguely or indirectly, leaving your partner to guess your exact meaning, and perhaps becoming angry when he fails?

As you develop the habit of listening to yourself in a more attentive manner, your spontaneous mode of self-expression will become clearer. Your partner's responses may come to reflect this change, and your overall patterns of dialogue will begin to improve.

3. Make written notes to expand your objectivity and fine-tune your awareness of the subtleties of dialogue.

After you have a conversation, jot down a summary of the content and, if you can recall the exact words, put them in writing before memory fades or distorts. Your immediate perception of what is said will sharpen when you form the habit of recalling bits of dialogue word for

word. In fact, you are likely to discover that your recall im-
proves, even when you don't have a chance to make notes,
because the habit of writing trains you to listen well.

As you review the resulting material over time, previously obscure themes and patterns will emerge with
clarity. Furthermore, you will gain sensitivity to how a
phrase can suggest different meanings at different times.
You may come to understand better why your partner
took your meaning a certain way or come to see the limitations of some of your own spur-of-the-moment interpretations.

4. Think of listening in terms of what you are not doing.

Effective listening requires your concentration, your
complete energy. When you listen with focus, you are not
busily formulating what you will say next or, worse,
making your mental grocery list; you aren't glancing at
television or humming a song or answering the telephone
or watching someone across the room, or staring into
space, lost in your own inner world.

*5. Find role models whose manner immediately invites disclosure
from others.*

What characteristics do these people have? Their tone
of voice, facial expression, and gestures indicate un-
mistakably that they are totally receptive to the one person they are listening to. Notice that open people are open
both ways—open to others' feelings as well as open about
their own. Observing the components of their receptivity and analyzing their absorbed interactions will guide
you in developing your own personal style of healing listening.

*6. Practice the magic of absorbed listening, intense eye contact,
and concentrated presence.*

Your facial expressions, nods of your head, and posture should indicate that you are hearing, understanding,
and feeling what your partner is saying. By inviting and

supporting open responses from your partner, these practices alone will deepen your level of communication.

You may protest that such gestures are not natural to you and will seem rehearsed. However, as you practice them, they will tend to *become* genuine and spontaneous, just as your learning to walk or talk has. Appropriate feelings tend to follow where sincerely motivated changes in behavior lead.

Going Around His Defenses

Would you be more likely to open your emotional entryway to someone who came at an appointed time, knocked gently, and identified his mission, or someone who yelled "Let me in," and beat on the door?

If you forcibly confront your man's defenses, he will feel *more* vulnerable and will be *less* likely to let go of them; defenses are actually shored up by direct assault. If you do manage to crack his shell confrontively, he is likely to protect himself immediately with new defenses.

For instance, perhaps you notice that he is unusually critical of you when he returns from playing golf with his father. Suppose, further, that you have observed that his father is often harshly critical of him. In such a case, he is probably displacing his frustration and hurt with his father upon you. Yet his feelings of intimidation by his father are exactly what he *cannot* let himself see. While this pattern may be obvious to you, his own motivations remain obscure to him; that is the very nature of defense mechanisms—to keep ourselves unaware of our own protective maneuvers, to avoid knowing about ourselves what we cannot bear to face.

Your first impulse may be to respond aggressively: "Every time you play golf with your father you come home in a hostile mood. I haven't done anything to call forth this treatment. It's about time you get over your fear of your father and stand up like a man!" Such direct attack is likely to result only in further defensiveness on his part. After all, he might fear that he isn't a man, that he can't act like an adult, that his father is a bigger person than he is, that he has no right to speak up for himself. After all, his father was a big man when your partner was two feet tall. He may *know* better, but that's what he *feels.* When you challenge him, he feels even more like a mouse, compelled to *prove,* to himself more than to you, that he is not afraid. You could indeed have a desperately resistant man on your hands.

Now, what could you do to *go around* his defensiveness? For starters, when he begins to criticize you after he comes home from golfing, listen calmly as he tells you all that you have done which you ought not to have done, and what you have left undone which you ought to have done. Once he finishes, let it go—send it up into the sky on a mental balloon! For your own integrity you really must not *continue* to accept attacks, but you can do it once or twice, with full awareness that his anger has nothing to do with you. Tolerating offense temporarily as a strategy to turn things around may appear as if you are taking his unjustified heat; you are actually rising above it.

Later, another day, when he is in a better mood, bring up the subject of his father. Enable him to tell you in more detail how these outings go, what is said and done, what might be irritating him. Ask, without a tone of judgment: "Is something about your father bothering you? Do you go out with him because you enjoy it or because you feel that it's your duty?" At this point, you do not counteract and defend yourself against your partner's displacement of anger upon you. You *focus on what is going on with him.*

You might say: "I've come to dread your golf outings with your father, because you seem down when you get home. I'm wondering if it's something about your father. I know how critical he can be and that would certainly get me down." All of this is true as well as empathetic.

These are among the wisest, most therapeutic moves

93

you could ever make. Through such a gentle approach, you may enable your partner to recognize his own defenses and discover what they protect him from, freeing him to arrive at more constructive ways to fill his needs. This is essentially the process of going around defenses. As he gains insight into his relationship with his father, his necessity to displace his hurt and anger upon you may vanish and he may be able to face his problem and work it through.

Create an Atmosphere of Trust

A perception of emotional safety is your partner's first requirement for undefended talk and creates the context within which dialogue can take place. You can establish an atmosphere of trust by demonstrating that:

94

1. You will not betray your partner's confidences.
　　Confidentiality is the most elementary component of trust. Your partner must know when he bares his heart that he is speaking only to you, that you will not discuss his private disclosures with anyone else.

　　Unless you are in a personal crisis, in which case there may be valid reasons for needing to let others know about the particular segment of your life with your partner (for example, you are in therapy or are afraid for your personal safety), there are compelling reasons for keeping your partner's revelations private. One, of course, is the effect upon your relationship if he discovers that others know what he has said only to you. This knowledge, in turn, affects your interactions as a couple. Even if he never knows, *you* know, and your knowing changes the contact between you.

　　Also, if you are trying to reconstruct a damaged relationship, the fact that others know your secrets exerts a pressure which complicates the task of developing more trust toward each other. When in the presence of these other people, the two of you are likely to feel self-conscious anxiety as if you are under observation.

2. You will not store up secrets as weapons against your mate.

When you feel backed against a wall, when other resources seem unavailable, and you feel that you must defend yourself, you might be tempted to retaliate with the weapons against him which your mate has previously given to you. Don't do it! This man is your companion, not your enemy.

3. You will not morally condemn him.

One of our greatest trepidations when we disclose hidden feelings is that we will be judged harshly and rejected. All of us have done things we regret and dread to tell. When the impulse to condemn your mate—for words, feelings, or actions—comes over you, remember that his very disclosure represents an act of courage. In revealing his inner truth, he has demonstrated the very trust you are trying to encourage. If you can do so with sincerity, express your admiration for his bravery and your gratefulness for his trust.

95

With these three matters assured—you won't divulge confidences; you will not store up secrets as ammunition; you will not condemn him, making moral judgments—you create a climate of trust and safety so that your man can peel away his mask.

Your sense of trust in each other weaves through your whole relationship—it doesn't come from only a few well-chosen sentences. Once he is convinced that you've put an emotional net beneath him to cushion his fall, your partner might find the courage to reveal himself.

The comfort and security required for undefended dialogue are established over time through healing experiences. The techniques in this chapter for healing listening

and emotional connection constitute a significant beginning in your move as a couple from isolation to intimacy.

A general atmosphere of trust encourages verbal
touch. Now that you are aware of the broad principles
that inform such a climate, you can begin to focus on specific patterns of communication that tend to inhibit, and
those which invite, verbal connection. The next two
chapters focus respectively on the common "WordTraps"
that deflect further disclosure and the healing "Word-
Bridges" that encourage it.

℀
WordTraps
How You May Be
Discouraging Disclosure

What is most critical is that each person see how he contributes to his own problems in his very efforts to solve them.

Ari Kiev

. . . disclosure is often what transforms our relationships from superficial, stereotyped, role-playing arrangements into unique, deeply fulfilling ones.
Adler, Rosenfeld, and Towne, *Interplay: The Process of Interpersonal Communication*

IN A SINCERE EFFORT to be supportive, you may actually cut off your man's tentative efforts to express his feelings. Imagine going to a psychotherapist who, when you laid out your problems, said, "Cheer up, it can't be that bad!" or "You shouldn't feel that way," or "Oh, you don't mean that!" No one would seriously consider this kind of reply as effective therapy, yet most of us use such shallow phrases in our everyday communication in a supposed effort to encourage our mates. It won't work in therapy, and it won't work for you either, to fall into such Word-Traps.

When you think you're being receptive, you may actually be participating in encouraging your partner's emotional silence. Women are typically conditioned to hide behind a veneer of "niceness." WordTraps are time-accepted "nice" remarks, trite communication-stoppers, verbal platitudes which inhibit feeling-level talk.

When you presume to read your man's mind, to tell him how he feels or how he *should* feel, what he should do or not do, even what will happen when he does it, you are *participating* in the problem you set out to solve.

The underlying characteristic of all WordTraps is that they invalidate your partner's words and feelings, telling him, in effect, that what he says is not true, does not make sense, is the wrong way to feel, or has no value. Regardless of your benign intentions, WordTraps are not reassuring.

When I teach about WordTraps, my students often adamantly defend their use, at least at first. As Deborah Tannen, author of two bestselling books on male-female patterns of communication, writes, "No matter how dissatisfied people are with the result they are getting, they rarely question their way of trying to get results. When what we are doing is not working . . . we try harder by doing more of what seems self-evidently the right way."

As with any firmly conditioned behavior, we scarcely notice our speech patterns. If your man points out that you cut him off, you might protest that you were only trying to be supportive or to continue the flow of conversation. While you may have been taught that such words are helpful to others, that they represent the "right thing to say," they may very well be your major contribution to your partner's silence.

Tony and Carmen

Tony and Carmen were a young, married couple whose difficulties with communication—which initially pro-

> ### Myth
> Our folk wisdom is that we reassure others by the use of "nice" clichés, empty phrases such as, "Everything will be all right."
>
> ### Consequence
> Intending to give support, we actually cut off communication with WordTraps.
>
> ### Reality
> Such platitudes are *not* reassuring; they invalidate the disclosures of others, and trivialize their problems, making molehills out of their mountains.

pelled Carmen to contact me for therapy—illustrate many of the pitfalls of WordTraps. Carmen complained that Tony never told her what he was feeling. She felt shut out and lonely. I asked her to describe an ordinary conversation in as much detail as she could.

The story she told was this: Tony was to speak at a convention. Unaccustomed to public presentations, he worried about it for months. To show me how supportive she had been, Carmen said, "I kept telling him it would go just fine."

After Tony made the long-anticipated speech, Carmen told me, he came home in an awful mood. By his own account, his talk was a disaster and he was very shaken about it: "I'm telling you, it was terrible! I'll never be able to show my face at work again." While Tony did not say "I feel . . ." nevertheless he clearly communicated his feelings of humiliation, disclosing his vulnerability. Yet, she missed these cues.

"What did you say to him then?" I asked. "Tell me the words you used and how he reacted."

Carmen began, "I said I was sure it wasn't that bad." Even with the best intentions, Carmen had not *heard* his feelings. Tony exploded angrily and stormed out of the room, yelling, "How do you know how it went? You weren't there!" Without consciously analyzing the conversation, he felt the impact of Carmen's invalidation of his perception as if what he thought was of no consequence. It was as though Carmen had said, "What you think and feel has no basis. I am the judge of reality!"

Having no idea where she went wrong, Carmen reflected that Tony was taking his defeat out on her. "And," she concluded, *"I really tried."*

When Tony told Carmen he wouldn't "show his face" at work again, that struck a note of fear in her heart. If Carmen had responded to the *feelings* Tony communicated—humiliation and dread of facing anyone at work—rather than to the literal meaning of his words, she might have enabled him to work through his emotion.

Carmen, a caring woman, was doing her best to be genuinely supportive, by employing words most of us habitually and automatically use when we want to be supportive. In reality though, she was derailing Tony with WordTraps, trying to make him feel satisfied with his speech, against his own perceptions. Carmen tried to *change* how Tony felt rather than *accepting* his true feelings. And, if he really had bungled his presentation, self-deception wouldn't have served him well. Without having the facts, Carmen tried to pacify him in a fashion that might cast doubt upon anything encouraging she might subsequently say.

As a result, Tony's confidence fell even further. Not only was he upset about his talk, he was resentful of his wife's apparent inability to view him as a rational adult, to allow him to discuss his failure, to feel *with* him and *for* him—to empathize. Carmen, too, began to feel increasingly unappreciated.

Of course, the incident was one of many which shut down feeling-talk for the couple. Tony realized that instead of being more relaxed each day after coming home, he actually felt greater tension. If Carmen had not decided to do something to break their pattern of poor interchange, the two of them, as time passed, could have lapsed into tense and bitter silence.

Instead of picking up Tony's cues, hearing the feelings he revealed, and asking questions to support further articulation, Carmen gave Tony hollow reassurance in the form of WordTraps, thereby effectively shutting down communication. Like Carmen, when you think you're being supportive and facilitating personal disclosure, you may actually be turning off your partner's efforts to communicate. The self-evident right way to give verbal support, which we have all learned, is, in fact, the wrong way. Even when he is talking about ordinary events, about which you are not anxious, when the stakes are no higher than they were for Carmen, you may actually silence your mate while intending the opposite. Every WordTrap can stop your mate in his verbal tracks.

The WordTraps which follow will be divided into three categories: empty reassurances, condescending phrases, and devices of domination. These examples will sharpen your sensitivity to the subtly undermining language you may use so that you can recognize your own personal idiom of invalidation—your particular repertoire of WordTraps.

101

EMPTY REASSURANCES

Avoid phony, empty reassurances when your man admits feelings of weakness, anger, or fear, normal emotions which we all feel at times.

Word Trap #1: "It will turn out OK. Everything will fall into place." "You'll get over it."
    Example:
MAN: I don't know what I'm going to do about letting my secretary go. She needs the job, but she is totally incom-

petent. It's really hampering the business of the office. [Although he never says one *word* about how he feels, *everything* he says is really about his feelings: sympathy, conflict, worry over his business, a need to do the right thing.]

WOMAN: Don't worry; things have a way of working themselves out.

The fact is, problems usually don't just "work themselves out." Failure and tragedy do happen, and even mundane matters have a way of tangling themselves up. By offering superficial and empty verbal supports, you show that you do not really hear the feeling being expressed to you.

We can't turn our minds on and off like computers, erasing "worry" from the page. Like Tony, this man will continue to fret; he just won't say so. The woman has, in effect, told him he is foolish to worry and that she doesn't want to hear about it.

He may become irritable as he tries to sort out his thoughts alone. He could become hostile because she doesn't understand or take him seriously or, as he may see it, care about what bothers him.

Word Trap #2: "Think positive."

Example:

MAN (A LAWYER): It looks as if tomorrow is going to be real tough. I'm not as prepared as I should be for this case. [Again, he doesn't say "I'm afraid . . ." or "I dread . . ." He does, however, convey both feelings in describing his image of the day to come and his inner state.]

WOMAN: If you think it'll be tough, it will be tough. You have to think positive. You won your last case, didn't you?

The man in this example can't wave a magic wand to transform his apprehension and, if he can't talk, he will become even more anxious. If he has the sensation of cracking under pressure, he needs to discuss it, pour out the pain. He is trying to cope by divulging his fears. Such disclosure is *the* most effective, potent method for coping, which will lead to more fruitful thinking.

His worries may be appropriate—he may, in fact, not be prepared, in which case it is likely that the day *is* going to be very rough indeed. If his partner wants to encourage him, the best thing she can do is hear him out. Perhaps he will convince himself that he can prepare further.

Who has the authority to say someone else should "think positive"? If you believe any expression of fear is to be avoided, you may constantly attempt to buoy up your man by telling him not even to think of the fears he is trying to tell you about. That might very well have been the message his parents once gave him. In response, your partner won't stop worrying, but he may stop telling you about it.

While an optimistic viewpoint can ease various crises, genuine positive thinking is not simply a recital of unrealistic expectations, which is counterproductive unless you have already taken practical steps to ensure the outcome. Positive thinking does not earn an "A" on a test for which you have not studied, nor will it repair a leak in a boat, or get a drunk driver home. And the admonition to "think positive" certainly doesn't give encouragement to someone who is upset.

Similar platitudes include remarks about how tragedies build character or how people beset by misfortune are drawn together (when more commonly the opposite is true).

Word Trap #3: "You have so much to be thankful for."

Example:

MAN: I don't know why so many bad things happen to me. Not only do I lose my job; now, with the car accident, every penny we have is down the drain.

WOMAN: But you have so much to be grateful for. You should see the people I work with at the homeless shelter.

Using this WordTrap heaps guilt upon him, implying that he has no right to focus upon his own problems when others are worse off and the world is full of misery. He won't feel that he has a right to complain; his verbalization of feeling has been cut off.

WordTrap #4: "It isn't that bad."

Example:

MAN (INFURIATED THAT PROPERTY TAXES ARE GOING UP): We'll move. I won't put up with this. What do we get for our money anyway?

WOMAN (QUIETLY): Oh, honey, it isn't that bad. You said we'd move when the city sold the lots across the street. You know you don't mean it. Besides, we get a lot for our tax money.

The taxes may not have been the single reason for this man's outburst; rarely is there one cause for any effect. He may have been passed over for promotion that day or found out that he needed expensive dental work. The tax matter may have been his last straw.

It doesn't matter that he is not saying everything he feels; he has hardly had the opportunity. He is, however, putting his feelings into words, not running his fist through the door. The soft-spoken woman thinks she is soothing his temper, while in reality she is patronizing him.

Perhaps this man *doesn't* actually intend to move; maybe he's just letting off steam. But telling him he isn't going to do as he says might precipitate his taking a stand he doesn't really want to take in order to make a point to his mate.

Word Trap #5: "Things could be worse."

Example:

MAN: Sweetheart, if my commissions keep going down, we can't stay in this apartment. I feel like a failure saying this, but the money just isn't coming in.

WOMAN: Oh, don't talk like that; things could be worse.

That things could be worse is exactly what this man is afraid of. Things do become worse if we don't deal with them as they occur. Wouldn't it be better to do something before the situation deteriorates? The woman in this example is cutting off a fine effort toward problem-solving communication.

If this man did wait, perhaps until they lost their apartment, his mate might then say, "Why didn't you tell me while something could be done about it?"

Word Trap #6: "Cheer up—let's do something else and get your mind off of this."

Example:

MAN (A PHYSICIAN): I'm wiped out. I've had it at that hospital. Did I go to school for ten years for *this*?

WOMAN: Everyone has work problems, honey. Let's go to a movie and get your mind off your problems. That'll cheer you up.

The man in this example made a clear introduction to talking about his feelings. Distractions might be relaxing *after* he's had a chance to declare how upset he is and to sort out his feelings.

Suggesting an immediate diversion communicates that your partner's emotions are trivial and intolerable and that you want to escape hearing about them. Suggesting that you both simply forget his mood implies that his feelings are not worth your time or his.

CONDESCENDING PHRASES

Eliminate words which imply that you know your partner better than he knows himself and that *you* know what he should do and how he should feel.

Word Trap #7: "You shouldn't feel that way."

Example:

MAN: I'm not spending any more time with your friends! All their husbands went to college. They treat me like a dummy.

WOMAN: Oh, dear, you shouldn't feel that way! No one is putting you down.

There is no such thing as *should* when it comes to feelings. Advising your mate how he *should* feel lacks insight and promotes guilt. Emotions don't respond to guidelines and limitations. Using the phrase "shouldn't feel" asserts that you are the proper judge of what is right for your partner to feel, and that emotions are logical and controllable.

It's healthy to have strong feelings, whether they're justifiable or not. In fact, it isn't possible to eliminate feelings by attacking their rationality. If feelings are denied over time they acquire a more destructive potency. When your man misses the opportunity to talk his feelings through, accumulated energy can lead to acting out.

Word Trap #8: "I used to feel that way."

Example:

MAN: Sometimes, I think if I have to listen to that kid cry for another minute, I'll just walk out.

WOMAN: I used to feel that way.

Ostensibly meant to show empathy, this superior and condescending comment implies that you have moved on to a higher plane of maturity. Your man will feel patronized. If he can tell you he is tempted to leave, and you listen, he is far less likely to do so than if he never spoke the words.

Word Trap #9: "What you're really feeling is hurt . . . (anger, fear)."

Example:

MAN: I'm furious about what Al did; I'm ready to punch him out.

WOMAN: What you're really feeling is hurt. You just interpret it as rage because that's more comfortable for you. Al has been your best friend for years.

Or:

MAN: I'm depressed. My boss sets these unrealistic sales goals for me and then when I actually meet them, he doesn't recognize my accomplishment.

WOMAN: It's clear that you're not depressed but angry. You've always resented him for being brought in from out of town when you thought you would get to be manager.

The woman in the first example interprets the man's anger as hurt, and the woman in the second example interprets the man's depression as anger (and then reminds him of an incident he would probably rather forget). Telling your mate what he feels is a violation. Even though pop psychology has advanced the view that we can know what others are feeling more clearly than they do, this patronizing ploy presumes that by some superiority of intelligence or telepathy, or merely by noticing his behavior, you are able to tell your man what he *really* thinks and feels even if it opposes his own insights. To make matters even worse, if he counters, "No, I don't feel that way," you might, in following this trend, accuse him of being defensive.

Word Trap #10: "You don't want to do that." "You don't mean that. If you do that, you'll feel bad."

Example:

MAN: My work is getting me down. I think I'll give notice and look for another job.

WOMAN: You don't mean that.

MAN: I'd rather be out of a job altogether than put up with this stress every day.

WOMAN: That would be a mistake. You'll be sorry if you do that.

She is not only advising him about how he feels; she is predicting how he is *going* to feel. Even if you are skilled at assessing your partner's present and future feelings, he needs to develop his own insight. Enabling him to do that is an integral and essential part of intimate communication. He will back off, understandably and justifiably, if he sees you as forcibly invading his thoughts. And if you foretell what he will feel, he may go out of his way to show you that you don't know everything, deliberately creating a secret emotional life.

Word Trap #11: "I know how you feel."

Example:

MAN: This has been the worst week of my life. My research project is a failure, and I don't think we'll get any more funding.

WOMAN: I know how you feel.

While you may aim to be empathetic, saying "I know how you feel" cuts off further disclosure by implying that it's unnecessary, particularly if your partner thinks you don't really know what he is actually enduring. Even if you have been in a similar situation, you may not know how he feels. We all tend to feel that what we experience is unique, that no one has ever loved as we have, suffered as much, had such intense emotions. And, in many ways, each inner experience, regardless of its trigger, is unique.

DOMINATING DEVICES

Change patterns of speech which shift your role from that of friend and lover to all-powerful figure. These Word-Traps consist of *styles of response* rather than words and phrases. Using such devices tends to place couples into power struggles. If you become the one who controls, you diminish your partner's power; this is not intimacy.

Word Trap #12: Avoid replies which don't directly relate to what your man has said or which redirect the conversation.

Example:

MAN: I'm worried about the income tax.

WOMAN: Me, too. I'm sleepy, are you?

Or:

MAN: I really need a rest.

WOMEN: Yes, you do. You're running late for your appointment, aren't you?

Or:

MAN: Sometimes I dread coming home. It's always so chaotic around here.

WOMAN: Busy little place, isn't it? Now, what you need is some dinner!

When your man begins to tell you how he feels, you may tend to change the subject by bringing up thoughts or suggestions of your own that are at best only remotely relevant. In response, your partner may feel that you are

109

attempting to dominate him by controlling the topic of conversation or by implying that his thoughts are not worthy of discussion.

Word Trap #13: Don't respond to his angry accusations with counteraccusations of your own.

Example:

MAN: I get furious when you stay up every night after I go to bed.

WOMAN: How do you think I feel when you spend more time watching TV than you do with me?

Or:

MAN: When are you going to have the carpets cleaned? I can't believe that you would ignore something I've asked you so many times to do.

WOMAN: *You* can't believe it?! As if *you* always do exactly what *I* want! Do you remember the last time I asked you to give just half an hour each evening to *your* kids?

Choose another time to air your own grievances. Otherwise, you cut him off in midstream. His feelings need to be explored. Remember, men often translate other emotions into anger; if he says he is furious, perhaps it will lead to a revelation of loneliness or rejection. Perhaps he is, in fact, angry, in which case he needs to express this feeling.

Word Trap #14: Don't tell your partner what to do or begin statements with "If I were you . . ."

Example:

MAN: I don't know how to handle this situation with the board of directors. It's unethical to go along with their new program, yet I can't afford to lose my job.

WOMAN: What you should do is confront them about it.

MAN: Don't tell me what I should do!

WOMAN: I was only trying to help!

Telling your man what he should do is another I-know-better-than-you-do message, which will cut him off rather than encourage expression and problem-solving. Even a faint fragrance of coercion is anathema to certain males. Even though many men tend toward inveterate problem-solving (especially the Hero), don't automatically conclude that your man wants advice or direction when he brings up a problem. It is better for you to assume that if he wants advice he will ask you for it.

If he habitually allows you to take over, his confidence in handling his own life may shrivel, as perhaps your respect for him will also. If you become his decision-maker, he may eventually blame you for his failures. It isn't your responsibility to find his solutions. Processing and deciding for himself strengthens his confidence and choice-making capacity even though he *will* make mistakes. Your choices for him would be just as prone to error.

Word Trap #15: Don't deny his perceptions.

Example:

MAN: That guy next door can't stand me. My relationships always end up this way. I start out OK and then, after a while, people just turn on me.

WOMAN: Oh, no, you always interpret silence as disapproval. That isn't how he feels at all. When we saw him at the party last week, he was perfectly friendly to you. You're misreading him. Sometimes I think you're paranoid.

One of the most patronizing replies to a person's declaration of feeling is to suggest that he is wrong to see things as he does, as if you are in sole possession of revealed truth and reality. Denying the validity of your man's perceptions probably won't convince him that he is wrong, and, even if you do persuade him, he may come to resent you.

If the man in this example had been allowed to continue on with his story, perhaps he would have been able to put events into perspective, identifying his own misperceptions. Perhaps his viewpoint was quite accurate; he may have been perceiving a pattern in his behavior that does elicit rejection from others.

Word Trap #16: Don't attack his defenses.

Example:

MAN: I have a job interview coming up tomorrow; it might be only a matter of weeks before I get hired.

WOMAN: You don't have to bluff with me; you know you're scared. That isn't a job interview tomorrow—it's just lunch with someone who may have a contact.

MAN: Everything's going to be fine.

WOMAN: You're just denying your feelings.

Defenses are the big guns of secrecy, thoughts and feelings buried so deep you can't remember where you put them. You aren't even sure you ever had them! We develop defenses to fool ourselves, to keep from having to face a reality which is too painful. Then the walls we build not only shut others out, they shut us in with our own demons.

When your man acts brave, calm, or cheerful in the face of a realistic problem, you must be willing to let him wear his protective covering for as long as he needs to. If you expose a feeling he isn't yet ready to deal with, he is likely to become even more defensive. Defenses can be psychologically necessary for a time. Besides, you may be wrong about what constitutes a defense on his part and what is authentic expression.

Word Trap #17: Don't question him in ways which he may interpret as coercive.

Example:

WOMAN: Why are you always so late getting home these days?

MAN: Thanks a lot! As soon as I walk in the door I'm being interrogated!

Often, men justifiably take offense at questions beginning with "Why do you . . .?" which they might take as being challenged or caught in the wrong. Questions starting with "Why don't you . . .?" imply that they aren't intelligent enough to devise their own solutions.

Word Trap #18: When he is telling you his feelings, don't instantly defend yourself.

In *Men Who Can't Be Faithful*, author Carol Botwin offers examples of how women feel compelled to defend themselves when their men tell how they feel. "If he says he feels neglected, you . . . tell him you were busy taking care of the kids . . . if he says [of another woman], 'She made me feel young,' [you] might respond, 'So you were acting like an old fool!'" Such statements qualify as Word-Traps. They cut off further disclosure by "turning the tables" and requiring the man to defend himself.

In each dialogue above, a man who was attempting to verbally convey his feeling was being cut off by a Word-Trap. Becoming familiar with these examples will raise the level of awareness of your own communication-inhibiting patterns of verbal response. You will begin to notice Word Traps in your own and other people's speech.

You will need time and practice to weed them out. Guidelines in chapters four and seven, such as note-taking, provide the means. The easiest way to cancel out one habit is to replace it with another—in this case, the supportive responses of WordBridges, described in chapter six. WordBridges will enable you to actively facilitate close and intimate talk, actually giving the support and encouragement you have intended to give when you fell into WordTraps.

CHAPTER 6

ର୍ଚ

WordBridges

What to Say to Help Him Open Up

*The most powerful resource we have for transforming
ourselves is honest conversation.*
Sam Keen, *Fire in the Belly*

*Feeling is an enemy only when one doesn't know how
to express it. And it is necessary to express it entirely.*
Henri Matisse

NOW THAT YOU HAVE focused upon creating the sense of
safety necessary for undefended dialogue, and examined
some of the ways you may be inadvertently cutting off
your man's tentative attempts to talk about his feelings, you are ready to learn WordBridges—supportive
responses which encourage further disclosure. Word-
Bridges are verbal connections, thought-bonds, which
get beneath defensiveness and establish emotional contact
in dialogue.

Using WordBridges will facilitate your elimination of
WordTraps. You can replace offending phrases with more
effective ones. Your brain can more readily *substitute* different, constructive words than merely remove destructive ones, leaving nothing in their place.

In chapter five, when Tony wanted to tell Carmen

how upset he was about his speech, Carmen effectively cut him off by using WordTraps. Now let's look at what Carmen could have said using WordBridges:

TONY: Carmen, it was terrible! How can I show my face at work again?

CARMEN: Tony, I'm sorry. Tell me about it.

By WordBridging in this very simple way, Carmen could have demonstrated that she accepted Tony's vulnerability and cared about how he felt. If Tony had been supported in pouring out his feelings, he may have been able to put the day's events into perspective. There would be other days and other talks. He was not washed up as an employee, much less as a person.

If Carmen's tactics had been different, Tony might have described how he lost his train of thought, how one employee talked to another during the speech, or how his boss walked out of the room fifteen minutes into the presentation.

Possibly he would have realized the response to his talk had reflected jealousy or a hidden agenda among his peers, or that he had been overly sensitive to someone's facial expression. Perhaps he would have decided to talk it over with a trusted co-worker, who could give him objective feedback.

Tony might still have concluded that he fumbled the presentation—an idea which Carmen seemed unable to entertain—but realized that did not make him a failure. If Carmen had used WordBridges, he could then have seen that she sincerely appreciated him, that even when he failed, he could count on her honest support.

As you study these guidelines and examples, keep in mind that simply memorizing specific words will not fulfill the spirit of WordBridging, any more than learning nouns and verbs will make you a writer. If you parrot therapeutic phrases without a tone reflective of the understanding behind them, they will appear to be stilted, rehearsed, and insincere. If you absorb the meaning of WordBridges and discover how they work, their intention will become a part of how you think and feel as you use them.

As WordTraps are means of invalidation, the underlying principle of WordBridges is unconditional encouragement. Words which sustain disclosure always have a courage-giving spirit, mirroring your empathy, your skill, your attitude, and your genuine love for your partner.

I divide WordBridges into two types: those which you can use to initiate conversation, and those used to respond to your partner when he begins to talk. The following lists of each type start with the simplest, progressing to those requiring more skill on your part and more openness from your partner.

INITIATING DIALOGUE

Use these WordBridges to initiate dialogue, preparing your partner to hear your feelings and participate with you in intimate communication.

WordBridge #1: When you want to talk, make an arrangement, not an attack.

Be direct. Giving your partner an advance request, rather than surprising him with your problem, reduces potential anxiety for both of you. Offering options on time and place decreases pressure, facilitates internal preparation, and diminishes defensiveness. No one likes to be taken by surprise; men, particularly, say they are sometimes at a loss for words when their women expect instant verbalizations.

Be mindful of your timing on issues which require time and emotional energy. Be sure that neither of you is worn thin emotionally before you start; that you will have uninterrupted private time; and that he is at least willing to hear what you have to say. *Ask* for dialogue with Word-Bridges such as these:

- Can we talk tonight about what happened when we went shopping?
- I'm feeling angry. Is it OK to talk now, or would you rather wait till the weekend?
- When can you take time for me to tell you about something that's bothering me?

WordBridge #2: Bring up only one subject at a time.
Tell him straight out what you would like to talk about.

- I'm worrying about the conversation we had over the weekend.
- I'd like to talk about our interaction last night with the kids, OK?

The following example represents the possibility of overwhelming your partner with too many issues at once: "We need to talk. I'm concerned about who does what in the house. We don't have enough time to accomplish everything that needs to be done. Recently, you've been coming home late from work, leaving us with even less time for household chores."

A more focused approach would consist of a statement such as: "I need to talk about how we're going to divide the housework."

The following example represents approaches which are too vague:

WOMAN: Can we talk?

MAN: What do you want to talk about?

WOMAN: I'm not really sure. It's just that you never talk to me.

A more specific response to the man's query is called for:

WOMAN: Can we talk?

MAN: What do you want to talk about?

WOMAN: Well, I feel that we don't have enough time to- gether anymore, and I'm wondering what we can do about it.

She isn't WordTrapping her partner by labeling him as neglectful; rather, she's taking responsibility for her own feelings and approaching him for cooperation in devising a solution. If you start with "Tell me everything you're thinking," "Let's talk about feelings," or "I need to talk about our relationship," and give no further clues, your man is unlikely to know how to answer.

If you don't know exactly what's bothering him, yet feel that your partner may be upset with you, try honesty: "I feel that there's something wrong between us and I'm not sure what it is. Can we talk?" Balance your lack of cer- tainty by stating your feeling that you don't quite know how to begin.

WordBridge #3: Keep on track.

After introducing a subject you want to talk about, stay with the issue at hand and finish with it before mov- ing on to other matters. If you attempt to deal with too many issues at once, you get mired down and never really settle anything.

If your partner brings up other issues, gently retrack with statements such as:

- I'll remember that you want to talk about my doing errands when you're at home on Saturdays. For now, can we just talk about how we divide the housework?
- What you're saying brings up all kinds of other issues in my mind, but we should probably get this problem

taken care of first, and come back to the other issues later. OK?

If you have stored up a great deal of debris in your relationship, you may both have a tendency to erupt when you start to talk about even relatively innocuous subjects. In such cases it will require discipline to pick one angle, one piece of grief, one problem, or one feeling, and talk it through without tossing in the aggravations and agonies of your common history. *You have to be selective to be effective.*

If your partner insists on diverting the conversation, you may need to discuss his problem first and return to yours later, in order to ease his anxiety.

WordBridge #4: Take responsibility for your own feelings.

When you approach your partner for discussion of a specific issue, even if you are enraged, say what you feel; do not blame him, judge his actions, or label him. Simply describe your emotional response to an act of his. Statements in which you give an account of your own feelings can stimulate discussion, and they are less likely to raise your partner's defensive wall.

A statement such as "You are thoughtless to have forgotten my birthday again" is an example of blaming and labeling. Whether or not he forgot, whether or not he was careless of your feelings, your saying so will immediately fortify his defenses and block further exchange. You will sound as if you are blaming him, thus cutting off his freedom to express, perhaps even to apologize. Regardless of your justification, accusing him will terminate conversation. Explain your feelings as they pertain to his specific actions: "I feel hurt that you didn't bring me a birthday gift."

Some statements, which begin with your feeling, still place a label upon your mate, thus calling out his defenses. For example, "I feel angry that you *flirted* with that woman," or, worse, "You *always flirt* with all the women." WordBridging in this instance would consist of a statement like, "I'm very angry that you talked for so long to that woman."

When you attempt to engage your partner in open discussion, your aim is not to blame him but to express your feelings and to examine the problem.

WordBridge #5: Offer your own vulnerabilities.

When faced by your partner's silence or refusal to talk, you may have to take the first risk and leave your own sensitive areas exposed.

This move may be more difficult than you anticipate. Many women are not entirely open as is generally supposed; we are just closed about different areas than men are. Sidney Jourard's research shows that there is a reciprocity in disclosure, a relationship between what people are willing to disclose and what others disclose to them. Disclosure invites disclosure. If you want your partner to be open with you, start by being open with him.

When you tell your man something about your feelings that leaves you vulnerable to ridicule, anger, or disapproval, he can feel safer in talking to you. Few can resist

121

Myth

While men are verbally closed about their feelings, women are quite open about themselves.

Reality

Women are probably more open than men, but we are not entirely open as is generally supposed; we are just closed about different things than men are.

Consequence

We sometimes don't let ourselves know some of the things we dare not tell; we need to work on our own closedness, not just on our men.

the invitation of such a defenseless gesture. Revelation of your own secrets constitutes a kind of emotional collateral, assuring your partner that he can, in turn, offer his undefended reality. Start with the least risky issues:

- I'm feeling really insecure right now. Maybe being pregnant is part of the problem. I wonder if you can understand.
- I'm uneasy about this situation and I just can't keep it to myself any longer. I hope you can see why I feel this way.
- I need to tell you something. Please, will you listen to all of it before you say anything? I'm afraid you'll be hurt.

With no effort to persuade him to do the same, expose feelings you have about yourself, such as anxiety concerning your job, your aging, your appearance, your grief over the loss of a parent, your response to a controversial book you're reading, and other issues of emotions that are not closely and directly connected with your relationship. Express your interest in hearing what he has to say about similar subjects.

More delicate problems require that you be prepared for emotional fallout:

- I told you I went to my mother's when actually I went out to lunch with Jeffrey. I feel guilty about deceiving you and I need to talk with you about it. Please listen until I finish.
- I need to tell you something and I'm afraid you will be angry. I listened to your phone call last night.
- I feel ashamed to say this: I've been faking with you for a long time. I'm having problems becoming aroused.

(Notice that she does not WordTrap him with statements such as "You don't arouse me," or "You don't turn me on.")

RESPONDING

These WordBridges provide responses which will encourage your hesitant partner when he is making even small steps in the direction of disclosure—when he falteringly, reluctantly, begins to tell you how he feels. Taken in sequence, these WordBridges begin with a minimum of threat, moving progressively toward more sensitive areas.

WordBridge #6: Ask him what happened.
Ask your partner to describe what was said and done in an interaction in which he was involved. This kind of WordBridge is compatible with many men's customary style of describing events, as opposed to feelings:

- What happened at the banquet?
- And then what happened?
- What did you do? What did he do?

And, when he has responded to your invitations:

- What did you say?
- What did he say to that?
- What did you say then?
- What else did he say?

WordBridge #7: Ask what he thinks; show interest in his *perception.*
Now that you've asked him what happened, move along to a deeper level of dialogue. He may at first be more comfortable exposing his thoughts than his feelings:

- Have you thought of what you'd like to do about this situation?
- What do you see as your strengths in this?
- What did you think when he said that?
- Did you think I was being pushy?

WordBridge #8: When he speaks spontaneously, reinforce him; support further disclosure.

To encourage him to talk more openly, as he begins to reveal his thoughts and feelings, develop the habit of asking "listening questions" and making comments which support additional disclosure on his part. This is possibly the most powerful WordBridge of all.

- Please tell me more about that.
- Please help me understand better what you're saying.
- I'm sorry, I don't quite understand what you mean yet; can you tell me more about it?

As your partner gradually moves closer to opening up about his feelings, encourage him in that direction at each conversational step:

- Oh, I can just see their faces when you said that!
- That must have been really scary for you to say.
- I appreciate your telling me about that.
- Thank you for trusting me with that. (You acknowledge that he may have feelings of vulnerability without directly alluding to them.)
- I think I understand.

WordBridge #9: Listen for the sake of listening.

With the kind of problem that can't be gone around and must be gone through, listening caringly may be all you can do—and it may be extremely effective. If your man says, "It wouldn't do any good to talk about it" or, "You probably don't want to hear about it," WordBridges such as the following can be helpful:

- I *would* like to hear about it.
- Maybe there's nothing I can do, but I would be glad to listen.
- It might help just to talk; try me.

WordBridge #10: Facilitate solutions.

If your partner is working on a decision, open up dialogue about multiple alternatives. Instead of suggesting options or volunteering assistance, offer questions and comments which stimulate his ideas:

- If we talk this problem over, probably you can think of other possibilities.
- Maybe if you tell me about it you will be able to see it in a new light.
- What are the risks (drawbacks, possibilities, the worst thing that can happen)? What do you have to lose?
- Have you ever faced any problem like this one before? What did you do? How did it work out?
- What else have you thought of doing?
- What plans are you considering?
- What have you already tried?
- Have you considered saying anything?

WordBridge #11: Ask him about his anger.

Men are often more comfortable revealing anger than exposing other emotions. So, to establish the least threatening line of questioning about his feelings, ask him about his anger.

- Were you angry?
- I would have been furious if he had said that to me.
- I can certainly identify with you if you were angry about that.
- I think almost anyone would be enraged in those circumstances.

WordBridge #12: Know when to be quiet.

Learning rhythm, cadence, tempo, and timing in dialogue with your man is an accomplished art.

Women's patterns of speech tend to be more dialogue and less monologue than those of men. Women routinely punctuate each other's long discourses with questions, comments, and reactions. Even if two women find themselves talking at the same time, they may hear and understand each other nonetheless. Sometimes we find it can even be fun.

Whereas women may perceive themselves as giving signals of affirmation, men sometimes feel they're being interrupted. As a man talks, he may take moments of silence to collect his thoughts. Let these be; he needs to set his own pace. If he seems to be struggling, not knowing how to continue, you might respond with your eyes and face and emit sounds of response, the "hmms" which mark concentrated attention. Be sure, though, to give him time to finish. Nods and sounds of comprehension might persuade him along; just don't cut him off at his point of hesitation and rush in with your own comments, responses, or consolations. As Deborah Tannen says, a man expects a listener to be quietly attentive; when you offer a "steady stream of feedback and support" he may be annoyed.

WordBridge #13: Ask him how he feels.

When you feel that both of you are ready to move to a more intimate level of talk, ask him—in your gentlest manner—what his feelings are:

- I'm concerned about you. If you can tell me how you're feeling, I'd appreciate it.
- Did I do something that you feel hurt about?
- Are you feeling something you think I might not be able to deal with?
- As tough as it might be for both of us, can you tell me what you're feeling so we can do something about it?
- I need to tell you some of my feelings, but first could you tell me how *you* feel now?

If you have an intuitive sense about what your partner may be feeling, you may be in a position to ask the empathetic question: "Are you feeling sad because . . . ?" or "Are you angry that I . . . ?" Even if you are off the mark, your compassion, your evident desire to comprehend rather than condemn, will, at the least, show him your loving intentions. (But make sure that you don't fall into the WordTrap of *telling* him what he is feeling.)

Asking him directly about his fears may threaten him, since men are usually conditioned to be ashamed of such supposedly weak feelings. Handle his tentative disclosures of fragile feelings with the gentle assumption that, of course, like all human beings, he does have fears, which are not only acceptable but inevitable—and that you love him even more for his candor.

WordBridge #14: Thank him for being open.

If he starts to utter words that hurt you, admit your pain, tell him you will need to deal with your own feelings later, then affirm his willingness to make sensitive disclosures:

Examples:

- Even though it was hard for me to hear, I appreciate your telling me that. It must have been hard for you to say.
- I see why you were afraid to tell me. Thank you.
- I can handle your anger, and I'm glad you told me about it. I have a chance now to change the situation.

WordBridge #15: Fight fire with water.

There may be times when you feel that you are not an appropriate target for his anger, but, to encourage his efforts to be open and honest, you can choose to resist the temptation to fight back, attempting to dampen the flames of his wrath rather than fuel them with your own fury.

If you throw everything in your emotional arsenal back at him, you will surely escalate the encounter. Alternatively, when you support him in expressing his charged emotions, he is more likely to finish up by being affirmative toward you. While you verbalize your receptivity, you are also likely to defuse an explosion:

- I am willing to listen to your anger and try to understand.
- I'm having difficulty with what you have to say, but I want you to keep talking.
- I want you to say whatever you feel—even if I get upset. You are certainly justified in feeling as you do.

WordBridge #16: Check your impressions. Check his out as well.

♌

128

When he is trying to tell you how he feels, struggling to get his point across, periodically repeat as accurately as you can what you *think* he is saying, not telling but *asking* him to verify your perceptions. One way to get at meaning which is not obviously and clearly stated is to reflect what you think is being conveyed and ask if you have it straight. Ask him to confirm your feedback or to clarify for you if you miss the mark:

- Is this what you mean . . . ?
- I think you're saying . . . Is that right?
- So do you feel (hurt, angry, frightened)? Sounds as though you do.

Repeating and paraphrasing what he has said clarifies his emotions for him as well as for you. And if you are upset by what he is saying and want to discuss your feelings about it, first be sure you are clear about *his* meaning. Wait with your feelings while you absorb all that your mate is trying to say.

If you senselessly parrot his words, as in pop-psychology clichés such as, "I hear you saying you are angry," he is not likely to feel understood, but rather to be put off. So that he can feel accepted and comprehended, carefully summarize—in your own words—what you believe you are hearing:

WOMAN: So, let me see if I understand: all your life you have felt you were doing things someone else's way and you began to feel you had to do it your way even if it turned out wrong. Is that what you mean?

WordBridge #17: Refine your awareness of your partner's subtle efforts to disclose his feelings.

Pay attention to his underlying feelings. Listen beyond content; listen for meaning. Probably your man is expressing emotion without the vocabulary of feeling-talk. You may not quickly identify his subtle attempts to deal verbally with an emotional issue, particularly when it is disguised by male-oriented idiom. Consequently, you might not respond in ways that facilitate further disclosure. For instance, if he tends to express his other feelings in the form of anger, you may close off in anxiety once he begins to talk.

As you listen, remember that fear and hurt may underlie his evasive words. Be open to the subtleties and resonances in his speech. Hear the feeling he is expressing rather than the literal meaning of his words. Tuning in to learn what he means is different from assuming that you already know.

Chances are you will have to filter through a lot of narration and description—events, daydreams, self-deprecation, or boasting—before you begin to hear his feelings. As you become more attentive to his expressions, gestures, and tone of voice, you can develop the skill of hearing what is not said, the reading between the lines of verbal communication.

As you learn to listen actively, as you begin to perceive the questions and emotions which are not overtly articulated, check your intuitions with your partner as you learned to do in WordBridge 16.

I do not intend to give the impression that you should always be on the lookout for hidden meaning behind every word. Simply be aware that none of us always say exactly what we mean. Listening between the lines of oral communication is a delicate and difficult area in which to sharpen your skills. Give yourself ample time. If you don't get it right away, you can do better next time.

Of course, real-life couple conversation is neither so clean-cut nor so brief as the phrases and snippets offered in this chapter; ongoing dialogue is complex and doesn't usually come in neatly separated packages as it necessarily must in written illustrations.

Consequently, while brief examples may suffice to illustrate the use of WordTraps and WordBridges, you will need a great deal of experience to absorb the tone and flavor of how to keep your dialogue flowing. If you are at a loss for what to say in the midst of a complex verbal interchange, remember the simple principle underlying all WordBridges: words which sustain disclosure always have a supportive spirit.

℃
Double Exposure
Exercises for Couples

*I start my story in the middle and move in both direc-
tions . . . There's a weight off me. I said it all out
loud and the world didn't come to an end . . . it
wasn't as bad as I expected.*
> Michael Dorris, *A Yellow Raft in Blue Water*

*When ironing out conflicts, many women feel, "The
marriage is working as long as we can talk about it."
Husbands think, "The relationship is not working if
we have to keep talking about it."*
> Aaron Beck, *Love Is Never Enough*

EARLIER CHAPTERS HAVE PRESENTED tools which you can
use on your own, ways of facilitating your partner's verbal openness that don't require active involvement on his
part. If you feel comfortable with and accustomed to the
methods you have learned, you can now move into a more
active two–person process. Ideally, you will enlist your
partner's participation in this next series of exercises, intended to open further the lines of communication between you.

Inviting His Participation

It is unlikely that a truly closed man is going to be whole-hearted about taking part in the exercises presented here. (His worries are partially justified; advice for women in books and magazines is often biased against males.) You might attempt to involve him by mentioning that you are trying to improve your own communication skills, explaining, if you can sincerely do so, that you need to understand yourself better and to listen more caringly.

"*I* need to change" certainly generates more receptivity than "*You* need to change." And, in fact, your first goal must be to change yourself. Saying that you need his help in changing and that you realize your need to listen more effectively is practically irresistible.

While the processes in this chapter are structured for couples, a very reluctant partner's tension and self-consciousness can be defused if you informalize the exercises by simply bringing up their topics—an alternate approach which will be demonstrated in specific instances below.

Proceed slowly so that your partner can see how you improve your own skills. Once you have started to listen effectively to him, chances are he will feel more secure working with you on communication. By opening the door, you give him a chance to walk through it, *if* he will. He must know that he is not being coerced; the choice is his.

Childhood Messages: A Place to Begin

A good place to start is with a low-key exercise on family messages. Earlier, in chapter three, you read about common family patterns affecting communication. Now, if possible, involve your partner in exploring the family messages about talking which were absorbed by each of you in childhood. You both will be more comfortable in talking about emotion by beginning with feelings which predate your relationship and thus do not directly involve each other.

You might stimulate discussion by constructing a "fill-in-the-blank" exercise on paper:

When the going got rough, my family _____.

Each of you can take a few minutes to think and jot down whatever comes to mind. Some of the phrases frequently used include "fought," "split," "clammed up," "talked," "pulled together," "drank," "cried," "took it out on each other," "yelled," "became violent," "found someone to blame," and "pretended everything was fine." Think in terms of both verbal and nonverbal communication. Your families' characteristic behaviors involved either the use of words or an avoidance of talking. Consider what effect their behavior and words had on your patterns of verbal interaction.

133

Next, talk about what you've written. Perhaps your partner will be more open if you speak first. Then ask him what messages his family gave him.

Most of us feel somewhat self-conscious when first participating in such personal exercises. If you anticipate resistance, you need not pose these questions directly to your mate. Perhaps he will be more responsive if the question comes up in normal conversation. You could casually introduce these ideas when you are both in a relaxed mode rather than setting out in a way he may perceive as contrived.

Exposing your own vulnerability first, you might say something like: "I've been reading this book and one of the questions is how our families influence the way we talk . . . or don't talk. I know in my family no one talked very much about anything. I grew up in virtual silence. I was quiet myself, and very tense, but I survived that way. When I made an innocent statement—sort of like 'I don't see any clothes on the emperor'—someone always jumped down my throat. So sometimes now I am too inclined to just keep my doubts to myself."

An introduction such as this requires a good measure of insight on your part, as well as ready articulation, and suggests that you are willing to take responsibility for your patterns of communication. By revealing first, you have provided security for his disclosures and a specific and recent model to follow in trying to recall his own experience. Your partner may respond with a "me too" statement. If he doesn't, you can ask him: "Do you remember anything like that in your family?"

If an even more casual introduction is appropriate to your situation, you could abbreviate the message: "Reading this book makes me think of how I grew up in a family that didn't talk. I think that still affects my ability to tell how I feel." "From things you've told me, it sounds as though your family got very quiet in a crisis. Is that usually what happened?" Or, even more briefly: "Oh, boy, this book gets to me. Just like my family." "What did your family do when things got rough? My family fought."

If you think your partner might *enjoy* talking about his early experiences, a simple opening question such as "When you were a child, did the people in your family talk to each other very much?" may suffice. Then, using WordBridges, you can invite disclosure of the themes of this exercise. Prepare to do a lot of listening if your partner is enthusiastic. This technique is not a trick; this is how good feeling-talk can start.

Starting at Both Ends of the Story

Perhaps you have a pervasive sense that you are disconnected from your partner, that you are existing in separate compartments, not sharing, and your contact has become stagnant or tense. You may want to discuss your relationship without knowing where to begin. How can you initiate deep discussions? There are two basic choices of approach. The first involves beginning with present feelings and moving backward into the past. The second involves beginning with the past and moving forward in time to the present situation.

BEGINNING WITH THE PRESENT

Start with current emotions and move backward, tracing events and feelings leading to your present situation. Talk over the "here and now" as clearly as you can, then move back in time to explore when and how your present feelings began. (You may be able to figure out what went wrong, or to uncover a specific precipitating event.) Don't look for a culprit or attempt to assign blame; simply recall and discuss feelings and events.

When dealing with a particular current issue which is relatively separate from the debris of the past, this quick approach may be all that you need, and, in any event, makes an *effective starting point*. When you simply want to open things up, it can also be a useful jumping-off place.

Example:

WOMAN: I feel that we are growing distant from each other. [Because there is no finger-pointing, this is less defense-provoking than, "I feel more and more distant from you," or "I feel that you are more and more distant from me."] I've thought about it and I'm not angry about anything; it's nothing you've done. [He can relax his vigilance and quit waiting for the axe to fall.] I can't quite figure out when it started. I'm wondering if you feel the same way.

MAN: Yes, I guess so. [He isn't denying that something is amiss and he isn't saying, "Everything will be all right." Even though he may be a man of few words, he has affirmed that his feelings are similar to hers.]

WOMAN: I felt that things were great on my birthday.

135

MAN: Yeah, we had a wonderful time. [Now she knows that he perceives the recent past much as she does.]

WOMAN: What do you remember about how we were last Christmas? [No longer will he be able simply to agree with her. She is throwing the ball to him and asking him for his own feelings.]

MAN: Well, I can't remember off-hand . . . but come to think of it, we had an argument coming home from your folks on Christmas Eve.

WOMAN: Oh, yes. I thought we'd settled it right away, but now, looking back, I'm not sure.

MAN: My memory is that the atmosphere was kind of cool on Christmas day when my family visited. [While they are simple and brief, his words nevertheless indicate that he is sensitive to her moods and that he does remember and reflect upon them.]

136

This couple is now "off and running." They can tell each other how they felt on Christmas day and recall other memories. Although they almost certainly will need numerous discussions in order to develop mutual insights about what is happening in their relationship, the process has begun.

Beginning With the Past

An alternative to beginning with present feelings is to start with your earliest memories as a pair. There is a major advantage to this more lengthy approach: thinking and talking about early romantic times injects warmth and hope into a more recently conflicted or stagnant relationship. Reminiscing, both of you may begin to feel some of your original tenderness and passion once again.

After they have laid out their problem, I sometimes ask a troubled couple that I am counseling to "take me back to a better time." I ask about their initial attraction, about what went *right* back then, and what they still like and appreciate about each other. I find that, even when they are deeply distressed, a couple nevertheless may relate the story of their meeting with laughter and knowing glances at one another; they *do* share wonderful secrets. It seems that, for a time, they are back in that early phase of eager romance, telling *their* story together, not *his* against *hers.*

Here is an example of a couple using this approach on their own:

WOMAN: I feel that we're increasingly disconnected from each other. I know that all relationships have their highs and lows, but I think this phase has gone on too long.

MAN: Since when?

WOMAN: I'm not quite sure.

MAN: Then how do you know it's been too long?

WOMAN: I just feel that it has.

MAN: I understand what you mean. I guess this is just the way things are after you're married for a while.

137

WOMAN: But I don't want it to be that way for *us* . . . remember that trip we took the spring after we got married?

MAN: Yes, that was a wonderful time, like a honeymoon, but . . . things happen. We both have too much on us now; I guess we can't expect to stay like that forever.

WOMAN: Maybe not *all* the time, but at least *some* of the time. Is there anything written that says we can't still be in love? I still love you.

MAN: I still love you, too. But I wouldn't know how to begin to change things.

WOMAN: Well, we both remember that trip with nostalgia. Can we talk a little about it and then try to see what happened after that? The loveliest thing I remember is . . .

In order not to divert couples from the problem at hand, I ask them to re-enter the past only after I have heard about their present conflict, and the weaknesses and strengths of their current contact. We return to the past in order to clarify their present.

This sequence might also serve as a valuable structure for you. A major advantage of starting at the beginning is that you return to high points in your history, stimulating both hope and incentive for recovery of your early intimacy. Recalling intense love is usually a nonthreatening place to begin to explore your relationship and enhance your bonding.

It isn't necessary to choose only one of these two approaches; you can weave back and forth between present feelings and past experiences as therapy ideally does. Connecting threads already exist between your immediate perceptions and those of your past.

Discover Your Boundaries

138

Sam Keen has spoken of establishing and cherishing "inviolable boundaries; to respect our separate sanctuaries." Outlining the boundaries of your personal communication—what to reveal to each other and what not to reveal—is a major issue connected with healthy needs for privacy. Every person has the right to a measure of emotional solitude. Such boundaries allow us to keep our personalities separate and distinct, to maintain our sense of individuality, by marking the place where one self leaves off and the other begins.

In your intimate relationship, it is neither wise in terms of deepening your communication nor psychologically cleansing to always and totally bare your mind. Being truthful with your partner does not require expressing everything you feel and think. Intimacy is not so much a matter of revealing all as it is the *freedom* to be open.

As Robert Frost said, "Good fences make good neighbors." Respect for each other's individuality and privacy is part of the courtesy we must extend to our dearest and closest just as we normally do to strangers and acquaintances.

You can ease fears of merging, of losing your sense of individuality, by affirming and reaffirming your separate identities, confirming his rights, and yours, to unique personhood. We have probably all known someone who says of a partner: "He won't *let* me cut my hair," or "She *makes* me come home right after work." Partners who maintain a sense of individuality will not inhibit each other's simple freedoms in this way. Their message to each other is, "It's not up to me to let you go out with your friends. I can tell you my feelings; the decision is yours."

To be intimately connected, you must maintain your separate selves. If you give your partner genuine assurance of his and your individuality, he is more likely to feel secure in telling you what he feels without worrying that he will be absorbed by you or that you will oppose rather than accept his feelings.

The more individuated you become, the more distinct your personalities, the more your fears of being consumed diminish, and the freer you become to belong to each other. With intense bonding comes enhanced individuation. *Establishing* boundaries is itself an exercise which precipitates heavy emotion. In identifying boundaries, you each need to answer *for yourself* the question of what *must* be revealed in order to sustain your intimacy. Although we all need private psychological spaces, *hiding truths in ways which have a detrimental effect on our relationships diminishes our inner integrity as well.* Deception hurts the deceiver as well as the one who is closed out.

Perhaps the two of you have opposing ideas about privacy and openness, the limits of intimacy. One or both of you may be practicing a double standard, insisting on knowing the very kinds of things you keep to yourself—a sort of "What's mine is mine; what's yours is mine, too."

Needing to know everything about our partners with-

> ### Myth
> Close attachment and individuality are often considered mutually exclusive opposites. We commonly believe that when we are bonded to another person we must give up some of our individuality.
>
> ### Consequence
> In our struggle to establish our individual identity, we may resist belonging and intimacy.
>
> ### Reality
> There is no conflict between attachment and individuality. On the contrary, the more individuated you become, the freer you are to be bonded. We can form deep attachments *only* when we are well-grounded as individuals.

out disclosing very much about ourselves renders even more difficult the essentially complex process of agreeing on what need not be shared.

Each of you may feel you have a *right* to know all by virtue of your relationship, becoming incensed if denied omniscience in regard to the other. Asking questions can then sound more like a cross-examination than a sincere effort to know. As one young client of mine said of her lover, "When I ask him about his day, he thinks I'm grilling him on his whereabouts."

Boundaries usually have more to do with privacy than with actual secrets, centering on, for example, whether you routinely call each other's offices, read each other's mail, or linger in a room listening to one another's phone calls. Privacy simply for the sake of solitude often becomes an issue, especially for the partner who chooses more solitary time. Some people are extraverts, who glory in the presence of another person, no matter what they are engaged in. They prefer to read with their partners in the same room, leave bathroom doors open, or talk on the telephone to a friend while playing cards with their partner; they readily share space and belongings. Others are introverts who prefer to be alone for activities, keep personal items separate, and are energized by solitude. (If you and your partner are not matched in your inclinations, a fine start for understanding yourselves and appreciating each other's differences is found in Keirsey and Bates, *Please Understand Me.*)

Thus, no set advice about boundaries applies to everyone. You and your partner need to reach a cooperative comfort zone. You both need to consider and discuss with each other issues such as: What boundaries of privacy trigger anger or fear when crossed? What sorts of "invasions" call forth hurt feelings and insecurities? What private territories provoke shame or guilt when opened to view by each other?

The following questions will require in-depth evaluation:

- *If someone confides in you, are you responsible for telling your partner?* The guiding principle in such matters is the degree of relevance to the partnership. Your best friend's affair need not affect your partner or your relationship, and thus need not—and perhaps should not—be divulged. On the other hand, your teenaged daughter's revelation that she is pregnant almost certainly must be revealed (although even there you may have to weigh her trust against his).
- *Do you need to reveal everywhere you go and everything you do?* There may be a difference in boundaries between lunch with an old lover and shopping with a female friend. (And what about how much you had to drink the other night and the fact that you dented a fender?)
- *Under what circumstances should you account for what you spend?* How relevant to your relationship was that expense? Decisions about discussing money are affected by how the two of you have set up ground rules for expenditures: whether you have discretionary funds;

whether your partner wants to know; whether the cost exceeds your ability to pay; whether one of you sees luxury where the other sees necessity.

- *Regarding sexual feelings or fantasies, what do you* not *want to talk about, and why?* Are you reluctant because of shyness, apprehension about getting hurt, or fear of hurting your partner? Do you really want to listen to details of his attraction to other women, and does he really need to know of your fantasies about other men? (Here I refer you to Harriet Lerner's *Dance of Deception* for further reading.)

CLARIFYING YOUR BOUNDARIES: AN EXERCISE

Each of you selects what you want to keep as private territory and what you greatly need your partner to disclose. Carefully consider *why* you each feel the need to know about a particular subject and whether it is an essential part of your relationship. Together you attempt to design an arrangement which satisfies both of you, requiring an examination of your individuality and your intimacy.

To structure your boundaries, fill in the blanks to sentences such as the following:

> In order to feel _____, I need to know _____.
>
> In order to feel _____, I need to (do)(be able to) _____ without discussing it with you.
>
> In order not to feel _____, I need to be able to _____.
>
> I do not want to talk about _____, because _____.
>
> Examples:
>
> In order to feel (secure) . . . (safe) . . . (loved) . . . (close to you) . . . (respected) . . . (like an individual), I need to know (how much you earn) . . . (when you will be home) . . . (more about the relationships you had before we met).
>
> In order not to feel (violated) . . . (angry) . . . (shut out), I need to be able to (call you at your office) . . .

(know in advance when you make plans that don't include me).

One of you may ask for openness in an area while the other counters with a need not to disclose. Here is an example of a couple resolving such a conflict:

MAN: In order to feel that you trust me, I need you to tell me the essentials of your past.

WOMAN: In order not to feel violated, I need to be able to select what I reveal about my past.

MAN: But you tell your therapist everything. In order to feel that I'm valuable to you, I need to know whatever is important enough to you that you tell someone else.

WOMAN: I don't believe I should have to tell you about the years before I knew you. I don't want to talk about my childhood because I become too upset to function.

MAN: I understand that, and it's OK with me. It's not your childhood that's bothering me.

WOMAN (BRISTLING): In other words, the *roots* of my problems are inconsequential to you, but you want to know about my adult relationships with men. Is that it?

MAN: I guess it is.

WOMAN: I'm afraid to talk to you about that. You might change your feelings about me. Or someday you might throw it in my face.

MAN: But I've told you those kinds of things.

WOMAN: I wish you hadn't.

MAN: But I told you because I feel that we need to know each other, and part of that knowing involves our history.

WOMAN: My childhood is my history, too.

MAN: Yes, and someday you might tell me more about it. Somehow, you make it sound like there's something wrong with me for wanting to know about your past romances.

WOMAN: Why do you want to know? Help me understand that.

MAN: I'm not quite sure. I don't know if I can put it into words, but I'll try.

Now this couple is on the right track in spite of their conflict. If he can help her to understand why he wants to know, and if he can assure her that he will accept whatever she tells him, she may eventually be able to speak more freely to him, or he may become secure enough that he no longer has the need for details.

This couple could benefit from discussion about why she wishes he hadn't told her about his romantic past. Understanding each other's motivation for needing to know or for wanting not to divulge is sometimes more important than the secret in question.

There must be give-and-take in working out boundaries; the process is ongoing. The areas you don't verbalize represent where you perceive your personhood as having its borders; these edges are fluid, not set in concrete. Consequently, your limits may change over time.

If you value your primary relationship, you are unlikely to create much material which must be carefully guarded. However, there will be a great deal which is never told simply because of time restraints and other logistics of living.

Tape-Record Conversations

You can enhance your listening capabilities and your verbal skills by recording your conversations. Having no way to hear yourself is like not being able to look in the mirror to check your clothing and makeup. How can you know what needs to be changed? At first you may feel awkward or embarrassed by taping, but you both will probably become more relaxed as time passes.

Because taping may be particularly threatening, the

issue of your mate's readiness to participate is raised once again. If he will feel violated by being recorded, then set this exercise aside. Don't record him secretly; openness cannot be expanded by subterfuge!

Whether you and your partner listen to these tapes together or you hear them alone, do not use the recordings as evidence or ammunition to prove a point about your *partner's* style of communication. Concentrate on catching your own slips, analyzing *your* response patterns, noticing when *you* fall into WordTraps.

See if you can write more effective versions on paper. Talk to your partner about what you found your mistakes to be and ways you might improve your responses to him. He may or may not reciprocate with insights of his own. That is his choice, too.

Reading Together

To stimulate dialogue about emotional issues, awaken memories of old scenes, and put you in touch with current feelings, read something together, something which is relevant to your relationship, which stirs thoughts and feelings about each other—such as this book. Among the many available books which would be excellent for such purposes are Maggie Scarf's *Intimate Partners,* Harriet Lerner's *Dance of Anger* and her *Dance of Deception,* Karen Horney's classic *Self-Analysis,* and Sam Keen's *Fire in the Belly.*

If you have two copies of a book or article, you could read separately, making notes in the margins, then talking about what the reading has called forth: associations, thoughts, and feelings you have experienced as you read. With one copy, you can, of course, take turns reading. Whichever way you choose, discussion after reading short segments is preferable to reading an entire book before talking.

Alternatively, reading aloud to each other can be a beautiful experience. One delightful thing about this practice is that it allows both of you to give each other undivided attention simultaneously. If you were fortunate enough to be read to as a child, reading aloud can re-create the feelings of coziness you might have experienced in childhood, and generate a sense of intimacy, trust, and relaxation.

Keep an Open Book

The Open Book is an ongoing exercise in which you start with a list of incomplete statements in a notebook; completing the sentences requires exploring your hidden emotions and the dynamic of your relationship. Finally, you and your partner read these statements to each other.

The Open Book provides an opportunity to practice all WordBridges. Writing in your Open Book also gives you a structure within which to communicate in a fashion less threatening than conversation, partly because it affords more time to make statements in a carefully considered manner.

The act of writing can also release some of your anger, lending insight and perspective on your feelings. By moving your relationship into focus at regular intervals, you enhance your awareness. Use the Open Book to express anger and other charged emotions. There need be nothing destructive about revealing your anger; on the contrary, expressing anger may be the most necessary thing you can do at certain times.

Emotions cannot be classified in terms of "bad" and "good." Therefore, instead of "positive" or "negative" I will use the terms "hot" and "warm" when distinguishing feelings for the Open Book. "Hot" emotions include fear, anger, excitement and other arousing feelings;

Myth

Verbally expressing anger and other charged feelings can have seriously harmful effects upon a relationship. This idea is based on the belief that there are inherently "positive" (desirable and constructive) feelings to be cultivated, and inherently "negative" (undesirable and counterproductive) feelings, which should be eliminated.

Consequence

Suppressing our expression and even repressing our feelings of anger can dampen our experience of passionate or tender feelings, rendering our relationships flat and phony.

Reality

Feelings such as anger are not negative in the sense of being undesirable within the context of relationships. Anger appropriately expressed can enrich relationships.

"warm" emotions include affection, gratitude, tenderness, and other calm feelings.

Below are some guidelines for creating and using the Open Book.

1. SETTING UP THE OPEN BOOK

Appropriately label separate pages of your notebook for expressing: 1) hot feelings toward your partner, 2) warm feelings toward your partner, 3) warm feelings you have for yourself, 4) things you would like your partner to do, and 5) concern about feelings your partner might have toward you.

Here are examples of opening phrases for expressing hot feelings toward your partner:

- I feel angry when you . . . [Not "You make me angry when . . ."]
- I feel frightened when you . . .

For expressing warm feelings toward your partner:

- I feel happy when you . . .
- I felt grateful when you . . .
- I am sad for you when . . .

For expressing warm feelings you have for yourself:

- I rejoice that I . . .
- I feel proud that I . . .

For expressing things you would like your partner to do for you:

- I would like you to help me by . . .
- I would feel grateful if you . . .
- I need your forgiveness for . . .

The following are examples of opening phrases for expressing feelings you are concerned that your partner may have about you:

- I am sorry that I . . .
- I am ashamed that I . . .
- I feel you'd be justified in being angry when I . . .
- I'm afraid that you feel angry when I . . .
- You could feel hurt that I . . .

2. FILLING IN THE BLANKS

When completing the statements in the Open Book, as well as when choosing your opening phrases, keep in mind WordBridge #4, which stresses the importance of minimizing your partner's defensiveness by refraining from blame. Carefully formulated statements neither insult nor demean your mate, and will reveal your feelings without requiring you to take on guilt for them.

Accepting ownership of your feelings in this way does not imply that you are at fault, that you singlehandedly generated the emotion in question, or that you chose your feelings. (The belief, currently in vogue in pop-psychology circles, that we cannot be stimulated to feel anger or hurt or any other emotion—usually expressed as, "I choose to be hurt; I know no one can make me feel that way"—is simply not valid. Holding ourselves totally responsible for any response we have can lead to detachment, denial, and numbing of emotion.)

Keeping in mind the principle of accepting ownership for your feelings, complete each statement in your notebook, in as many ways as necessary, by listing items you have mentally collected. Nonjudgmentally describe your partner's specific behaviors which prompt your feelings:

- I felt hurt . . . when you left this morning without saying good bye.

Myth

Current popular wisdom has it that we are entirely responsible for our feelings and cannot be made to feel anger, hurt, or any other emotion by anyone else—usually expressed as, "I choose to be angry; I know no one can make me feel that way."

Consequence

Supposing that we can choose our feelings can lead to detachment, denial, numbing of emotion, and diminished effort to change the situation.

Reality

This myth is a gross exaggeration. Emotions arise in interpersonal contexts; others have an effect upon us and we upon them. The words and actions of others are invariably a part of our emotional reality, just as a hot bath *makes* us hot and a cold bath, cold. What's more, it is natural and healthy to let yourself *feel* your feelings.

- I felt angry . . . when you said you didn't like the way I looked in my new dress.

A common mistake is to begin with a phrase such as "I feel . . ." but to follow it with a critical label. For example: "I feel embarrassed . . . when you behave like a fool" or "I felt hurt . . . when you were so rude to me." If you end your statement by blaming or labeling your mate, even if he is somewhat responsible, this may intensify his defensiveness and provoke greater anger, more rigid silence, or further withdrawal.

The words "always" and "never" are in themselves labels, implying a character trait rather than a particular behavior at a specific time, as in: "You always forget" and "You never let other people talk." Thus, you should avoid generalizing about his habits. Be specific, describing a single incident as it happened, without evaluation:

- I felt hurt when you said you didn't care whether I went shopping with you.

3. KEEP OPPOSING FEELINGS SEPARATED

Keep hot and warm feelings separate. To wrap a hot emotion like rage inside a warm one, such as affection, is to "sugar-coat" or "band-aid," as in "You are really quite patient most of the time, but I'm so angry that you blew up at me just now," or "I do love you, but I am furious . . ." This sort of "spoonful of sugar" dampens the hot expression and contaminates the words of warmth. (These layered messages can usually be identified by the word "but," following a statement of approval.) Subsequently, whenever you start to praise him, your partner will be prepared for the zinger that is to come. Mixing messages sacrifices their potency; the warm expressions can't be trusted and the hot ones lose their impact. If the two of you can develop a clearer, cleaner mode of communication, the hot emotion can be delivered as such without being diluted; the warm feelings can be offered—and received—wholeheartedly.

4. Notice the Balance of Hot and Warm Feelings

If the hot and warm statements in your Open Book are extremely disproportionate in either direction, this may indicate distortions in your style of emotional expression.

If you are frequently conscious of intense rage, and it dominates the statements in your Open Book, you probably have been withholding timely expression of it, causing a buildup of fury. Your pent-up heat may have obscured warmth and tenderness. Become aware of why you may be unable to *express* anger in an appropriate fashion.

On the other hand, if you write many confessions about your own guilt and regret, with very few angry or resentful ones, you may have trouble recognizing your hot feelings. Perhaps you cannot bring yourself to face your irritation, and, as a consequence, are unable to fully experience joy. If this is the case, you need to shine a light on the recesses of your mind, to recall incidents or attitudes of your partner's which could anger you.

In any case, the solution is to write out as much as you can of joy, sorrow, rage, terror, tenderness, love, grief, hurt—the full spectrum of human emotion.

5. Read the Statements Aloud with Your Partner

Read your Open Books aloud and respond nondefensively to each other's statements. Take turns: your partner reads a statement to you, then you respond; you read a

151

statement to him, then he responds. Avoid WordTraps; instead use WordBridges when responding.

Read and respond to each other's Open Books at least once a week, daily if possible. At first, the keeping and reading of these notebooks amounts to an emotional housecleaning. After you learn to express your feelings as they occur, not saving them up, there will be much less to write. Then I advise that you read and talk about both your Open Books at monthly intervals, no matter how things are going, until you both learn to feel your feelings clearly and to speak to each other spontaneously in the present time. Some couples enter a transition period during which they frequently leave love and appreciation notes to each other.

You need to deal with the stale segments of your relationship cycle in a timely manner with these self-therapy methods. There will be times when you need to re-examine your relationship and structure your communicating. When you notice that you are forgetting to talk, finding yourself too busy, or falling back into old, worn-out patterns, or when you are in a relational emergency, return to these exercises.

While you may at first feel awkward with this structure, practice will give you the flavor of it, which, as time passes, you and your partner will integrate into your own word-style.

You need not adhere rigidly to the forms in which the guidelines in this book are presented. As you absorb and apply the principles set forth here, your need for the "rules" as such will gradually decrease. Ideally, you will both relinquish defensiveness, disguise, blame, and guilt. Nurturing the spirit and intention that infuse the styles and techniques offered here, you and your partner will evolve new and more effective modes of communication on a moment-by-moment basis.

If your partnership is dynamic, there is always something new to be discovered between you, because as you grow individually, your relationship is transformed.

Our personalities are formed in the cradle of sound, of verbal symbol. Voices speak the words, the language. Words shape our minds, our spirits, our lives. Both speaker and listener, writer and reader, are changed by *verbal touch.*

Our very humanity is born from a sense of connectedness. Rollo May says, "The human being gets his original sense of . . . self out of his relatedness." Self-disclosure and self-discovery are inseparable, each leading back to the other.

CHAPTER 8

ᔍC

The Freedom of Forgiveness

Changing the Past to Create the Future

Each of us is subject to doubts and suspicions, flashes of mistrust. But a powerful current surges through us—an overwhelming need to touch and be touched, a powerful need to love and see that love returned. A need to transcend the awful solitude of this tomb called the body. A need to reveal ourselves, to unveil the deep secrets at last.

Gilbert Deering Moore

To perceive the world differently, we must be willing to change our belief system, let the past slip away, expand our sense of now, and dissolve the fear in our minds.

Gerald Jampolsky, *Love Is Letting Go of Fear*

ONCE YOU ESTABLISH THAT you are relating to the man you want to relate to, when you realize that the relationship is for better rather than for worse (which doesn't mean for perfect!), and you decide to stay in and work on the inner dynamic of your coupling, you will need to keep faith in the possibility of recurring transformation. That, too, is what faithfulness is all about—the vision that you and your partner can repeatedly transform your relationship, that both of you *can* really change. Forgiveness is based on the faith that this is so, that we can heal the past, that we can create a different future.

When you come down from the high of your first intimate dialogue, and communication returns to more mundane matters, you may become discouraged and think it was all a fluke, that your relationship really hasn't become what you momentarily thought it was in the excitement of your first breakthrough. "Can people really change and change deeply?" you may ask yourself. "Can I? Can he?"

We buy how-to books believing they can transform us from meek to assertive, depressed to joyful. We adopt abused children confident that we can erase old behaviors and feelings. We join Alcoholics Anonymous with reasonable hope that we can become sober citizens. I couldn't be a therapist if I did not share this vision of personal reformation.

To justify her hopelessness about change in her partner, a client of mine said, "I believe history is the best predictor of the future." I don't—not for individuals, anyway. Heaven help us if we are, as she believed, permanently stuck; our present choices would be meaningless. They are not. The changes we make today in our behaviors and feelings can recolor the past, enrich the present, and create a meaningful future.

Allen Wheelis, in *How People Change,* says, "The way we understand the past is determined . . . by the future we desire." Yet some of us bury the present *and* the future—we find it so nearly impossible to let go of our own woundedness and outrage at the past. We often become discouraged because we try to remake reality rather than work toward realistic change. With deep motivation, you *can* change your behaviors and you can change many of your feelings, while your personal essence remains intact.

155

While we want the abracadabra of magic, changing ourselves is more like evolution than revolution.

Participating in a dynamic interaction of relational forgiveness involves the whole texture of an authentic relationship. When your relationship is raveled and torn, you both have the opportunity to reweave the threads of past pain into the material of the present, developing an energy-creating relationship.

How is this done? If the two of you have followed along with me so far, if you have exposed your innermost feelings and he his—now what? Although intimate talk enhances your relationship, when you and your man move from being closed to being open, either or both of you may suffer a sense of injury from past silence, past secrets, or present painful disclosures. How can you keep from becoming embittered and blaming, or, conversely, from being a prisoner of self-punishment or guilt? To sustain your newly discovered intimacy, each of you must come to a position which is balanced and equal—accepting and accepted—neither permanently penitent nor stuck in resentment.

At this stage, if intimate disclosure and the relationship itself are to continue, you must learn the art of forgiveness, both of yourself and your partner. The multi-stage process of forgiveness outlined in this chapter is interactive and dynamic. It is a process of verbal communication as well as an entry point into future dialogue.

There are some wounds from the past, however, that may not be healed through verbal exchange alone, and there are some doorways to further intimate talk which require something other than words to be unlocked. The series of exercises at the end of the chapter can fulfill these needs, serving a number of purposes: to facilitate the process of cleaning up the detritus of the past; to provide the opportunity to cherish the present moment; and to facilitate your creation of the future of your relationship.

Forgiveness:
The Peacegiving Process

I speak here of forgiveness in the psychological sense. Usually, the concept of forgiveness is considered a religious or moral imperative, not a matter of subsequent trust, and carrying no implications for the future of the relationship. We speak of extending forgiveness even to people who do not care that they have hurt us or who do not participate in close relationship with us, who may even be dead. In the traditional meaning, you can forgive by your own act of will, whether or not the person you're forgiving accepts, cares, or even knows about your forgiveness. If your partner abandons you, for example, you might say, "I forgive him. I don't like him, but I'm not going to poison myself with feelings of hate toward him."

On the other hand, the kind of forgiveness discussed in this chapter is a continual transformation of your most intimate relationship, making it essential that you forgive both your partner and *yourself,* and that he forgive you and *himself.* If he is the perpetrator, you free him, and he frees himself, from the consequences of his offense, and you both release yourselves from the anguish of resentment. Both you and your partner must work through *your own* and *each other's* pain, blame, rage, guilt, shame, and anguish, thereby ceasing bitterness, absolving each other, and restoring trust.

This kind of Peacegiving forgiveness is restorative, redemptive to your relationship, requiring movement on your partner's part as well as yours, and it is reciprocal. Once it takes place you will *both* be in a relationship which is level and equal—neither guilty nor one-up. For the sake of your relationship, you need to extend forgiveness, toward both yourself and your mate; however, you cannot do it alone.

> ### Myth
> The only way we can forgive is to accept the moral and religious imperative to do so and, by an act of will, erase the past event.
>
> ### Consequence
> If we do not *feel* immediately and entirely forgiving, we believe we are mean-spirited. We find that a single act of "forgiveness" does not heal our relationships. Often we break off the relationship or hold a grudge forever.
>
> ### Reality
> Forgiveness in a relationship is not an event, but an ongoing process which can be accomplished through understanding, exploring, and implementing its stages. The three processes of forgiving your partner, being forgiven by him, and forgiving yourself are fundamentally related, and involve an overall transformation of thinking. One of them cannot take place without the simultaneous occurrence of the other two.

Forgiveness as Changing the Past

Those of us in need of forgiveness, especially when we are assailed by our partner's pain over what we've done or said, sometimes protest, "I can't do anything about it now; what is done is done and over. You can't change the past." Who would argue that point?

I would. My experience has been that you *can* change the past. We view our history in the context of present perception, and perceptions change. Recoloring the past is a continual facet of your relational experience, a way to reenvision events from the standpoint of a new context: the present moment.

Not only *can* perceptions change, they *do,* in fact, inevitably change with time. Your job is to shape that change in directions which work for you. Sincere, sane, sensible people can see things quite differently from each other;

Myth
You cannot change the past; it is over and done with and, if it is unpleasant, it is best forgotten.

Consequence
Believing we cannot change what has already happened, we sometimes fail to make attempts to recolor, refocus, and reframe the past, which continues to haunt us in the present.

Reality
In an important and personally meaningful sense, it really is possible to "change the past." The past continues to exist *only* through our recollections of it, the meanings that we assign to it, and its influence upon us. All of these forms of the past can be changed or recolored.

Consequence
By changing your perceptions, you can change the only reality that the past still possesses—its influence upon your present life.

159

and your earlier self had quite a different perspective from your current self. Someone you once loved passionately can finally leave you cold; "What did I see in him?" you ask yourself. A person who looked plain at first glance can become beautiful to you over time. The largest tree in the world which grew in the yard of your childhood, revisited years later, has shriveled to quite ordinary proportions.

Present perceptions color all memory; therefore we can recolor our mental pictures of past experiences by changing to the lens of present time. This truth lies at the heart of all relational forgiveness and reconciliation. When we recolor, we *see* events differently; and, seeing differently, we *feel* differently. There is no eternal truth in our initial perception of or reaction to events in our lives. We can say to ourselves, "At first I thought this, now I feel differently." That difference can be the wisdom we have acquired over time and through forgiveness.

Journal-keeping provides many revelations of how the past inevitably changes for us as time goes by. I find recording my thoughts and feelings in a journal to be enormously therapeutic for me. When I read my own journal entries made years ago, I see themes and patterns I could not see at the time, immersed as I was in the circumstances of that period.

Even more remarkable, when I remember an event, then go back and read what I wrote about it, my perceptions at the time of writing turn out to be quite different from the recollections I hold with the passing of time. My memories are bathed in a new light, colored by what I have experienced since, and what I am experiencing at the present moment.

The concepts of past, present, and future are images in your brain. Psychology writer Carol Tavris has this to say: "Researchers who study memory and the brain are discovering the brain's capacity to construct and invent reality from the information it processes. Their studies support what poets and novelists have always known: that the memory is not a fixed thing . . . It is a *process* that is constantly being reinvented. A 'memory' consists of fragments of the event, subsequent discussions and reading, other people's recollections and suggestions, and, perhaps most of all, present beliefs about the past."

A wise person learns from experience; a very wise person learns not to learn too much from experience. (The very wisest may learn from other people's experience!) As you lay filters of experience over those mental pictures in your memory, the patterns change—new features stand out, previously important details fade. And what you first see as a body in the road blocking your path may become clear to you as a heap of old rags over which you can easily step.

THE ROLE OF GUILT AND RESENTMENT IN FORGIVENESS

In order to undertake Peacegiving, we must understand the relationship between guilt and resentment (or anger), and the role of both in forgiveness. Harriet Lerner, in her bestselling *Dance of Anger,* says that guilt and anger are incompatible. Although I enthusiastically applaud her work, I see this particular point differently: my experience has been that if you cannot forgive yourself, you tend to blame the person toward whom you feel guilty. If you provoke feelings of guilt in your partner, he may resent you for it.

Ironically, when you feel guilty, you may need to express resentment and make firm but calm demands. And whenever you are resentful, find out what you feel guilty about, express it, and appeal for forgiveness. For example, you might feel guilty about not preparing full dinners for your partner each night, while you resent the fact that he does not participate in any cooking. Your own inclination may be to experience this feeling as *either* guilt or resentment—some of us internalize responsibility while others externalize it.

Guilt and blame are reciprocal aspects of the same phenomenon, mirror images, intertwined in our psyches, so that dealing with one automatically affects the other. In relational forgiveness you let go of both guilt and resentment. Since they share the same mental space, *each is made possible by the spirit of the other.*

Giving up your resentment frees you perhaps even more than it frees your partner; it is emotionally cleansing—not only to the one pardoned but, especially, to the one accomplishing this gracious act.

Elements of Peacegiving

The complex process of Peacegiving involves being forgiven, forgiving yourself (*accepting* forgiveness), and forgiving your partner.

Peacegiving is not an event, but a *multi-phase healing process.* It involves grief, a period of mourning for something which died in *you*—an illusion about what your partner is, a changed perception about what your relationship means, or a desire for a relationship perfection which does not exist. You realize these are gone; you grieve the loss of your dream of what might have been, what you thought was so, *your past view of reality.* You understand that part of your history as a couple must be rewritten, integrating whatever new knowledge you have. You don't let go of the grief until you've felt it, lived it, *lived through it, and integrated it,* and you come to peace. Peacegiving is peace receiving.

Peacegiving is not a matter of a moment's will, an immediate erasure. Such instant forgiveness is not possible in any *psychological* sense and, even if it *could* be done, it would be no particular blessing to your partner, who needs time to be receptive and to work on forgiving himself. Forgiving too much, too fast, does not eradicate emotion, but instead buries living remnants of resentment.

Pretending to "forgive and forget" in a flash is like adopting a new puppy the day after your old and beloved dog dies, or marrying again a week after you are widowed. Instant forgiveness is a contradiction in terms, just as instant recovery—bypassing the stages of grief or the steps of a recovery program—would be. That kind of pseudo-forgiveness often develops from a sense of self-blame or a tendency to be a martyr. Remember, healing takes whatever time you need. So forgive . . . but not too soon.

Here I will show you the elements of Peacegiving, from the perspective of both the forgiver and the forgiven. All of these elements involve the communication dimension of your relationship. As you will see, there is overlap; you need not fully complete one element before starting on another. For example, to fully examine your feelings, you must talk about them.

In illustrating the elements, I will use infidelity as an example of serious betrayal which may require maximum

Peacegiving, and describe what your feelings might be as you phase through the various elements of the process. The desired goal is that both of you reach a place of peace on the issue in question and that you thereby re-create your relationship.

Some underlying assumptions are made which distinguish *relational* forgiveness—Peacegiving—from traditional forgiveness:

For example, in using infidelity to illustrate the Peacegiving process, I am first assuming that the errant one of you has given up the "extra" lover. If that is not so, the emotional and practical aspects of that situation must be worked through, perhaps with a therapist, before you begin to engage in the Peacegiving process outlined here.

I am assuming also that you both have decided that you want to preserve and enhance your relationship and that both of you are willing to work to bring that about. That is not to imply that we ever arrive at a totally unambivalent position; it is only to say that you both make a commitment to each other, and that you are willing to *participate* in the Peacegiving process.

A client of mine was having an affair which was discovered by her husband. He told her that he knew, that he nevertheless wanted her to stay with him if she would renounce her lover, and that he never wanted to hear another word about it again. "From this time on, it will be as though it never happened."

Of course, this will not work. The affair *had* happened and the image of it remained frozen in their minds. This couple could not, in silence, find peace and recolor the past. She carried her guilt and he his hurt and bitterness. Without healing interchange, they became increasingly isolated from one another. Eventually, she found another lover. The problem which led to her first affair had never been dealt with. His refusal to even speak of the event buried the couple, instead of the past.

The elements of Peacegiving are demanding, sometimes excruciatingly painful, but no more so than a situation which needs forgiveness—in the illustration here, a breaking of faith in the relationship. In giving peace, it may seem that the forgiver is letting her partner get away with his faithless act. Actually, he already has. All you can do is work on how the two of you are going to handle it—whether your relationship will emerge stronger or weaker, more intimate or less.

WHAT IS RELATIONAL FORGIVENESS LIKE IF YOU ARE THE FORGIVER?

Element 1: Self-search.

Being the forgiver requires deep self-search, taking your feelings apart, analyzing and clarifying—not what you think you *should* feel or what others tell you to feel, but how you *actually* feel, the shades and textures of your emotion.

What might some of your feelings be? When you discover that your man has betrayed you, there will be anger, perhaps fury. Good—*you need your anger* for its motivating power. Anger gives you an advantage, energizes you to act, to take care of yourself. The adrenaline of rage pouring through your body may keep you from dissolving in despair.

You may be afraid to quit being angry with him, for fear that your vulnerability will deepen. Perhaps you have a history of forgetting too soon, of letting yourself be shredded too amiably, and becoming depressed. It is easier to act when carried on the wings of anger than when drowning in the muck of despair. There is a time for anger.

You may find that you deliberately engage your anger—perhaps you want a weapon to hold over his head. You may take secret pleasure in his misery. You may come to enjoy seeing your partner's discomfort as he tries to prove his love and make amends. That is natural—he has hurt you.

You may feel that your partner deserves punishment, deserves to feel guilty, that you deserve the upper hand, but eventually you must decide whether you prefer a relationship of love or of control, whether you want intimacy or, perhaps, that you would prefer revenge or martyrdom.

On the other hand, if you focus only upon what your partner wants of you, what you can do to gain his acceptance, how to avoid being rejected and abandoned, how to keep from offending and bringing down wrath—you might be inclined to forgive too fast. It is possible that you have never experienced the wonder of real love, neither giving nor receiving it.

You may have come to believe that the victim role is your only passage to acceptance, to belonging. This "lower hand" position can lead to depression, including its physiological manifestations, such as weakness, nausea, and trembling. You may fear to trust ever again.

These common positions perpetuate anger or a state of permanent penance. And so, if you are to enter into the Peacegiving process, you must employ the elements below. Talk with your partner *about* those feelings, listen to his truths, accept what he has to give—as vulnerable as that is likely to make you feel—and take part in the exercises which encompass behavior as well as words. These elements will facilitate your continued self-search.

As you persist in intensive self-examination of your own psyche, use the techniques outlined in chapters four and seven, such as the Open Book, or keep a personal journal of your feelings.

Element 2: Talk with your partner about your feelings.

This element particularly calls for all that you have learned in this book about couple communication, such as attention to time and place, to your choice of words, to your best WordBridging spirit. As you explore your emotions in an effort to see them clearly, you will need to talk,

expressing your rage, your sense of injury, betrayal—
with words and tears. Let your emotions pour out, or you
may find yourself petulant, sarcastic, sullen.

When I've been wronged, sarcasm is a great temptation for me. It comes easily; I'm good at it. When the
sharp words rise spontaneously to my lips, I know I still
have unresolved resentment. At such times, I need to release this hostility in more constructive ways—by *explaining* the misery I am experiencing. To win the contest of
words with a clever, biting remark is to lose the Peacegiving process, which is not a competition at all. Yes, the sarcasm *is* a real part of my feeling, but only its surface; hurt
and fear are the deeper emotions underlying my caustic
defense against my own experience of pain or humiliation. That pain must be expressed in order that I do not
further damage my relationship with unmitigated fury,
so that I can get in touch with my own emotion, and so
that I connect authentically with my partner.

Sometimes, if talking is too loaded, in order to be
clear to yourself and to your mate, in order to contain—
but not repress—the emotion which could overwhelm
you both, you might express your feelings in a letter to
him, and then talk to each other.

Element 3: Listen to your partner.

This is the hardest part; you will need all the skills described in chapter four to be a healing listener. By listening well, you can enhance your understanding of what
your partner was thinking and feeling when he committed the transgression against you. Listen to his story,
how it came to be, and what he now feels about it.

Don't wait for him to guess what you need from him.
Since he cannot go back and cancel the event, he may
think there is no point in talking about it. Tell him of your
intense need for his expression of remorse for your anguish. If you have been betrayed, you need—and your
lover needs for himself—a deep outpouring, a recogni-

tion from him of your pain, a passion that compares to the urgent craving that compelled him away from you. He needs to express whatever shame and guilt he feels, and you need to hear them. You need for him to pour out his agony *for your agony*—not simply his realization, in whatever way he labels it, of his own humiliation.

His sincere contrition is a cleansing move toward healing—for him and for you—and is required to recolor your perception of the event. When he expresses emotion, no matter your distress, wait with your response (in the way you have learned to do in chapter four) *if you can,* using your best WordBridges, so as not to cut him off. Your fears of vulnerability may prevent your feeling empathy for his struggle; you are grieving for yourself.

He may project his feelings of guilt or shame upon you, and so may lash out at you. *Those who feel guiltiest harbor the most intense sense of injury;* they are most ready to attack in defense.

To appreciate his position, recall your own feelings when you have been the perpetrator of an injury to someone else. Remember your remorse, how much you would have given to go back and erase the deed done. If your partner has ever forgiven you, get in touch with your own feelings of release when he lifted the crushing weight. *Let yourself feel empathy when it comes.*

Element 4: Accept his reparations.

Allow your partner to *take time* to restore your trust. Be open to his efforts to make things better, without keeping him on the hook as long as you can; after all, you are hanging there, too.

By accepting loving gestures that you fear may be setting you up for future injuries, you might feel that you are betraying yourself. However, being receptive to his efforts is a risk you must take for Peacegiving to have a chance. Trust *always* carries some degree of risk.

Once you establish that you are not loving too much in the sick sense of the word, that you are taking proper care of yourself, you can then afford to love and to listen and to forgive, thereby giving your relationship peace.

(If, over time, you find that your trust was misplaced, that you must take care of yourself rather than remain vulnerable, you will weigh again your original decision to forgive. Remember that relational forgiveness is contingent upon certain choices you and your partner make. If you come to realize that your partner is irretrievable to you, if you recognize that yours is *not* a situation which lends itself to Peacegiving, your choices might need to be reassessed.)

Each man will attempt to comfort his partner in different ways. Be receptive to any detail which he can supply to soften the blow for you. One man—once his other romance was over—said to his primary partner: "Eventually, when I was with her, I found myself thinking of you." Not potent enough to erase the wound, but certainly a little balm for the injury: he was, even then, beginning to turn back toward his primary partner; she was not being compared unfavorably.

Your contrite partner may come to you with kindness, tender gestures, great passion, love letters. As part of the risk of vulnerability required for intimacy, *dare to be receptive.*

Frequently, out of guilt or genuine remorse, a man buys his partner *things* to make amends. This tendency fuels jokes about men bringing flowers to their wives, who respond with, "What have you done now?" Men are programmed to gauge their worth by possessions—marks of status and achievement. Therefore, in considering how to restore himself to a favorable position, he may be inclined to think exclusively in terms of something money can buy. Sometimes men think material things are *all* they have to offer, just as women sometimes think all they can give is sex.

Some women, too, measure their own attractiveness by what and how much their men give them. Sometimes, women extort all the possessions they can in their partners' moments of regret. That is *not* forgiveness.

Whatever your man does in a restorative fashion, by seeing the intention, listening *to the meaning* in all his efforts to heal, you can let him know you are grateful for his remorse and assure him that you perceive the love, presence, and support which these things *symbolize*.

Element 5: *Temporarily set the matter aside.*

If, after a time, you find yourself unable to forgive, it may be that in talking continually you are repeatedly ripping emotional bandages off a raw wound. If this is the case, deliberately put the issue away for a while—depending upon the situation, perhaps for a month. Set a definite time to come back to it and make a fresh start at talking it through once again.

Meanwhile, work on other things, engage in distracting activities, talk about *anything* else. Gradually, the event will settle into the lower layers of your mind where it may lose some of its edge and allow you a measure of perspective. The event should be reopened later, unless you both *decide,* for any reason, that you are already prepared to extend Peacegiving to your partner and yourself.

Sometimes, when you and your partner have talked yourselves right down into a slippery pit, one of you may have enough love at the moment for a single loving gesture—a gentle, quick kiss on the lips, perhaps—which can brush away the pain. This *is* forgiveness.

Element 6: *Develop rituals.*

To examine your feelings, to drain the poison within you, to gain fresh perspective, to restore trusting feelings, you and your partner may need to engage in exercises such as those described on pages 175–181. Through the stimulus of these examples, you may, as a couple, be able to develop your own meaningful rituals—that is, acts which you establish and repeat purposefully over time.

Element 7: Reaching rapprochement.

There is a point at which the matter must be released, at least as an issue between you. This does not mean that the subject of your grievance is placed off-limits forevermore. You both will have remainders, reminders, and associations related to the event, although, in my experience, women are more associative in their thinking than men are. Our thoughts and feelings are set off by little things which trigger our memories—a street name, the sound of a fog horn, a song. At these times, you are vulnerable and may need to talk once more about the issue. With each open conversation, the pain can subside a bit more.

Rapprochement signifies that you both have rewoven a pattern—a recognizable new design. At best, the material of your relationship is stronger and richer than ever before. You understand to some extent the circumstances which prompted your partner to do whatever he did. You identify with your partner in any way you can. "I see what happened. Now you have *said* you are sorry. More than that, you have *been* so."

At this stage, you are giving each other peace and becoming a pair once again. Your perceptions are different. The past is in the process of being successfully changed. Take the time you need to become more secure and trusting—as you continue to recolor the past.

WHAT IS IT LIKE TO BE THE ONE FORGIVEN?

Element 1: Self-search.

As the one who needs to be forgiven, you also must engage in serious self-examination—a quest for complete *recognition* of the basis of your problem, not simply giving in to your partner's or anyone else's opinion about what you did. You may prefer to do this self-search alone, perhaps using your journal or seeing a therapist, or you may find it more productive to explore these issues with your partner, depending upon his capacity for healing listening.

Examine your deepest feelings. For starters, contemplate the roots of the event, why it occurred. Remember what was happening between you and your primary partner, feelings you were having then. Evaluate your need for high adventure as it pertains to the life you are living; think how you feel about yourself as a woman, whether you need constant affirmation of your own attractiveness.

Have you a history of self-destructive moves, a style of sabotaging your own happiness? Or do you feel that you strayed because of your partner's neglect? In this case, you need to establish that without recrimination. You can work these ideas out openly with your partner only if he recognizes that you are searching for answers, not delivering the final word on the matter.

If you have caused suffering for your partner, you may continue to treat him with abrupt rudeness, a defensive act against your own feelings of guilt. Consider whether you are genuinely sorry for what you did or simply sorry your partner feels as he does about it; either way you can express your emotion clearly, for what it is.

If you find that you cannot let go of your guilt, consider whether it might be serving as a continuing punishment for your perceived "sins and mistakes." For Peacegiving to work, you must eventually acquire a willingness to be forgiven. Ironically, being forgiven takes as much inner faith as forgiving.

Self-search is not something to be done as one step toward Peacegiving and then concluded. As you go through the elements of the process, you will continually be examining and re-examining your feelings, motivations, and behaviors.

Element 2: Tell your partner what happened.

Explain to your partner what happened, in as much detail as he desires or you need to present: how you feel—

guilty or grieving or frightened; how you *felt*—bitter or lost or confused. In helping him understand, be careful not to shift blame for the event to him.

If he did play a role in precipitating your behavior, you might let him discover that for himself through dialogue. If he seems not to apprehend his contribution to the event, tell him, in your best WordBridging manner: "I feel that your traveling, and your frequent comments on beautiful women, played a part in my need to prove that I am attractive, too. I need to talk about that." Other communications in which you take responsibility for your feelings without blaming your partner, as you learned to do in developing WordBridges, will further open his heart to you and yours to him.

Element 3: Convey your regret.

If your partner loves you and is deeply injured, he will need your expression of sorrow for his suffering and you will need to vividly express whatever genuine contrition you feel: "I cannot believe I did what I did. I feel as though some other self was acting in me. I cannot tell you how sorry I am, both for your agony and for my shame."

Element 4: Listen to your partner.

Hear what he has to say about the matter, over time, whenever either of you feels like talking about it. Don't simply turn the event into an unmentioned elephant in the living room, in the hope that he is not thinking of it. It does you no good for him to pretend everything is all right if it isn't. Not talking about important issues unquestionably contributed to the event in question in the first place.

Element 5: Change directions.

Determine not to repeat the event, and establish *how* you can avoid that behavior and how your man can support your efforts. This amounts to a psychological conversion, a transformation of heart and mind, a recoloring of your reality.

For example, if drinking played a role in your breaking faith with the relationship, you need to assess whether you have an alcohol problem which must be a primary target in your growth and change.

If your tension or temptation was centered in your workplace, consider a job change. If you fear that the same sense of isolation which drove you into an affair might rise up again at an unexpected moment, you must develop alternate ways of coping with loneliness.

Element 6: Redeem yourself.

The question to ask is: What can I give of *myself?* Think in terms of time, thought, talk, touch, tears—in other words, clear signs of your remorse, your love, of having thought intensely about your partner's wounds, needs, and desires, of your need to recolor the past.

In an amazing way, when one of a couple has been sexually unfaithful, there often comes a time during the Peacegiving process when their desire for each other becomes more intense than ever before. If you and your partner experience a profound and fierce renewal of sexual feeling, you may give him the gift of lovemaking. The bonding of this bittersweet yearning might well be the most vital element in your Peacegiving process. Peace, after all, need not be serene and quiet.

If you offer a material gift as part of your redemption process, make sure it's one which says, "I noticed what *you* said, what *you* want, who *you* are" (splendid criteria for any gift). Symbolic significance weighs more heavily than dollar value.

One man I know, in deepened commitment to his marriage, arranged for his wife to go with him to select new wedding bands on their anniversary—rings which represented a fresh phase of the relationship.

With the same idea in mind, some couples arrange second wedding ceremonies. For *your* sake as a couple, designing a ritual of beginning again can be Peacegiving. Too often the affair is known to others, whereas the renewed commitment is not. If you have friends you are very close to, people with whom you can be open, inviting them to celebrate the re-wedding ceremony with you, whatever form it takes, is appropriate and life-affirming.

A special surprise trip or gift which requires considerable time and thought to find or create especially for your partner can be significantly symbolic as a token of Peacegiving. One woman made a collage of pictures and objects from the couple's history, which left her mate in tears. Some have set aside a ceremonial time to burn objects connected with past events which they are recoloring.

Make reparations for whatever you did in whatever ways are meaningful. Exercises such as those on pages 175–181 enable you to forcefully and visibly communicate your remorse and receive forgiveness.

Element 7: Reaching rapprochement.

When the wound is healed, you both reach a place of atonement, where, for the most part, you *have* recolored your past. If you are the forgiven, you will *feel* released from guilt. Aware that you made a mistake, you will give *yourself* understanding: "I'm not continuing to beat on myself. I made a mistake—a big one—and I'm sorry. If I act from guilt, I will be introducing a destructive element into our coupling. I have done all that I can up to now to bring us healing and I will continue to live in a healing way."

The Peacegiving process—the recoloring of the past— is a gift you simultaneously give each other. Only people who take care of themselves can give—without *insisting* that their giving be accepted. They know what their limits are and won't go so far in giving that they are depleted and thus become resentful. Because they've dealt with their own guilt, they have no need to martyr themselves, and therefore they don't provoke others' guilt.

Exercises for Transformation: Present and Future

The following exercises were created for couples either immersed in guilt and anger, or going through the phases of forgiveness, which their previous verbal exchange had not completed. These exercises can be used to rebuild trust, to re-create your relationship, to stimulate intimate talk, and to sustain the excitement of being interconnected over time.

Couples with a serious sense of purpose about continuing reformation of their relationship often incorporate rituals into their daily lives. Rituals repeatedly establish renewal. They can be constructive and joy-filled means of recoloring the past and creating what is yet to come.

These exercises may lead you to discover and develop rituals in your daily lives, repeated acts involving parts of your body and brain different from those involved in speaking, and which therefore operate on a different level in restoring your relationship. Sometimes your unconscious takes over and makes changes for you—*the intention seeps down into the underlayers of the mind, focusing an image-activated change.*

These exercises, simple though they may appear, will invariably bring out feelings you haven't realized before. You may be jolted from your set attitudes or soothed out of your defensiveness; you will see yourselves and each other more clearly and your verbal communication will be enhanced.

OPENING TO VULNERABILITY

John needed forgiveness for an extramarital affair. While traveling in his business, he had formed a relationship with a woman in a city far from home. When his second wife, Darlene, discovered it, he tried to explain by saying, "I felt lost and empty all alone in a strange place." (And Darlene said *later:* "I feel lost and empty *now.*")

John had been totally unprepared when his first wife left him for another man. Instead of facing his vulnerability and loss, he anxiously plunged into finding a new partner right away.

Darlene was that person. Considering how hot and heavy their romantic beginning had been, she was totally stunned to learn that John had not been sexually faithful to her, particularly after only two years of marriage. She tried talking and listening to him. He kept returning to a single theme: the loss of his mother when he was eight years old. This loss, of course, had been replayed in his first marriage, deepening John's terror of abandonment.

Darlene realized then that there were empty places within John's psyche that had little to do with her or with the affair or strange cities or any other current factor in their lives. Not only did he have psychological hollows left from his mother's death, he had a burden of vengefulness toward his former wife with no place to lay it down. Darlene was receiving the psychic residue from both the unfinished grief and the unfinished vengeance. She persuaded him that they needed professional therapy together.

Darlene felt the need to do something active about healing their relationship. I suggested a process involving the theme of nurturance to enable John to fill up some of his emptiness: Darlene was to hold John every morning for ten minutes, stroking his head and humming to him without words.

She was aware of the common trap of being a mother to her man, and so she was concerned that this exercise would be too maternal. We discussed tender lovingness toward one's partner as opposed to dominating, criticizing, overnurturing, or other *negative* aspects of motherly wives. Once Darlene understood that tenderness is not necessarily motherly and can be appropriate in *any* close relationship, she was ready to participate in a process which actually felt very natural and pleasurable to her.

Every morning, sitting up in bed, she cradled John's head against her breast, caressed his hair, and rocked him back and forth gently while she hummed to him.

This simple exercise brought out feelings in John which he had no words for; sometimes he cried. After a few weeks, he realized an emotional security that talking therapy alone had not produced. Only then was he able to verbalize his feelings.

John thus gained insight into his own motivations in being sexual with another woman. He was deeply remorseful that he had hurt Darlene as he himself had been hurt by others. Through her he had found the comfort and acceptance he had been searching for in having the affair.

Once John reached this degree of insight by allowing Darlene to tenderly love him, a great change took place in his psyche, so that he and Darlene could complete the Peacegiving process, both confident that John had worked through his earlier urges to prevent abandonment.

177

LEARNING TRUST

Neela needed forgiveness for exploding unreasonably at her partner, Todd. One night he had arrived at her apartment two hours later than he had promised. Without waiting for an explanation, she harshly accused him of being "up to something." She screamed out all the nasty things she had mentally collected while she waited for him.

Todd tried in vain to calm her and tell her what had happened: he had intervened in a mugging and, after successfully intimidating the assailant, he had walked the elderly victim to her home. As the woman called the police, Todd waited so that he could relate what he had seen and done, as well as help her deal with the episode.

Still high on the euphoria of his courageous act, he had come to Neela's that night expecting to be welcomed as a hero. All the way there he was anticipating how he would tell her the story, how enthralled she would be, how she would share his triumph, how proud she would be of him.

When she started berating him the moment he came in the door, not letting him interrupt, he was at first shocked and then furious. By the time Neela had spent her venom, Todd was as angry as she was—angry that she would jump to conclusions and never give him a chance, angry at some of the "extras" she had thrown in, areas of contention she had never mentioned before.

Todd couldn't let it go. He was sullen and silent. A chronic state of tension gripped them both. Yet neither Neela nor Todd wanted to end the relationship. After several weeks of Todd's withdrawal and Neela's futile efforts to interrupt the tension and gain forgiveness, she asked Todd if he would consent to a few sessions of counseling.

At that point they made an appointment with me. They said their partnership had been satisfying before that night. Then why had a supposedly well-matched couple been unable to talk through the fury of a few moments?

We discussed the power of our mental pictures to set us up for being stunned when our partners' responses do not match our expectations. Both Todd and Neela had had images in their heads of what the evening would be like and neither was prepared for what happened.

I focused first on Neela. It was she who had originally

precipitated this crisis with her unwillingness to listen to Todd's story. I assigned a process to enable her to *allow* her own vulnerability: a silent walk on which she would be blindfolded and guided by Todd through the woods. It turned out that Neela was resistant to this exercise—she was very hesitant to put herself in the care of anyone else, even her lover. That was as I had expected. It seemed to me that Todd's late arrival had panicked Neela, so terrified was she of her vulnerability in loving and depending upon another person. If you want to find the one who is most tortured in a situation, look for the one who is most furious.

The very problem we were attempting to solve through ritual was the same one which made it almost impossible for Neela to participate in the exercise: *Out of fear, she fought off trust.* She had for so long covered her real feelings; her authentic but hidden emotion was buried even *more* deeply by her sudden torrent of words. Finally, we dealt with the trust issue sufficiently, so that she could give the ritual a chance.

They did the trust-walk every Saturday for six weeks. Todd led Neela along a quiet path, tenderly holding her and directing her steps. With his strong hands, he exerted gentle pressure to indicate that she should stoop down while he dipped her fingers in a cool, running stream. With no visual input to interfere, Neela could tune in to tactile sensation. Sometimes they sat on the ground for a while, absorbing the sounds and fragrances of the forest. Since Neela had for so long put down her sweet feelings, Todd's tenderness often proved overwhelming to her, and she poured out tears carrying torrents of emotion.

Coupled with our discussions of the background of her defensiveness, how she had become so hyper-independent, so afraid to let herself be taken care of, the trust-walk became a time of affection and silent touch which went beyond Todd's direction and Neela's dependence. Of course, this pair also needed the discussions we had, not only about the precipitating episode, but also about the roots of their personal inhibitions.

Todd, after all, had been unable to let Neela apologize immediately after the incident. He needed to work on his lack of capacity to *receive* reparations. As I had hoped, after a time the two of them decided to trade places and for the following weeks Neela guided Todd through the forest. Leading him on the trust-walk enabled Neela to express tenderness which she had no words or courage for in dialogue, to touch him in ways which, in effect, asked for Todd's forgiveness. For his part, Todd let down his guard and let go of his fear that Neela was going to hurt him again if she got the chance. At first, he had not been able to accept her overtures to peace, so shocked had he been at her explosion. So immediate was his pain, he was afraid to talk about it, protecting himself through silence and withdrawal.

Because Neela was learning to be vulnerable, *to trust,* Todd came to see that she could be *trustable, too.* In pain and panic an injured animal will bite the one it loves best; Todd recognized that Neela had lashed out at him from her own sense of injury and terror that he might abandon her. That made all the difference in his view of the episode, and enabled him to forgive and allow the restoration of their peace.

Through a combination of words and nonverbal exercise, in light of their new understanding of their own and each other's fears and needs, they had recolored their perceptions of the event.

YOU SEARCH YOURSELVES; YOU QUIET YOUR SPIRITS

There are two exercises which can reach into the depths of your emotion and your love for each other:

The first is to periodically schedule an hour or more for talking. Take turns being the speaker for half the allotted time, with no interruptions or response from each other. Then change roles.

While you are being the silent partner, you may want to make a few notes to remind yourself of points to which you can respond later. In that way, you don't have to hold distracting thoughts in your mind while your partner is going on to another topic. Instead, you can practice focused listening, using skills you learned in chapter four. When you are the talker, you can tell about yourself, about your partner, about the two of you, about feelings, dreams, hopes, hurts, delights, about anything you choose.

You each experience being listened to individually and being able to say whatever you want without interruption. This exercise is one method of addressing the self-search and the telling and listening elements of Peacegiving.

Another meaningful exercise which you may be able to establish as your own continuing ritual is to come together in a quiet place, for an hour or so, and be totally silent. Perhaps you will cry. Almost surely you will touch. You might simply hold each other. Without words.

This lovely practice embodies the elements of conveying remorse and redeeming yourself, and, finally, solidifies and celebrates rapprochement.

Although these exercises are not "real life," in the sense that they happen on their own or that the roles you play are your everyday self, they are nevertheless *real experiences*. The fact that you consciously created these circumstances in no way makes what happens to you less real than the often accidental happenings of everyday life. Exercises and rituals have additional power, not less, as a result of their purposeful creation. *Your mind records what your body acts out. Your psyche and your body will remember. You may then have recolored the past.*

If your partnership is dynamic, there is always something new to be discovered between you; as you grow individually, your relationship is transformed.

Restored and forgiven, can the primary relationship ever be the same as it once was? No, we are never the same again. Sometimes I think we never were "the same" in the first place. For our memory colors in the outline of what has been. Life is change. Perhaps, though, having each lost fragments of your selves in the struggle, you can create a vibrant new dance together. This book has instructed you in the basic steps. The dance is your own.

When you engage in what Sam Keen has called the "sweet agony of dialogue," instead of talking just to be understood, to express your feelings, you will be talking because word-exchange is one of the most stimulating activities two people can engage in. Over time, intimate talk transcends its original purpose as a means and becomes an exciting end in itself, as it may have been in the hors d'oeuvre stage of your relationship. You will find that you are not talking so that there *will be* intimacy— talking *is* intimacy, the communication of spirit to spirit.